# How Can the Mobility Air Forces Better Support Adaptive Basing?

Summary Analysis, Findings, and Recommendations

DAVID T. ORLETSKY, JEFFREY S. BROWN, BRADLEY DEBLOIS, PATRICK MILLS, DANIEL M. NORTON, JULIA BRACKUP, CHRISTIAN CURRIDEN, ADAM R. GRISSOM, ROBERT A. GUFFEY

Prepared for the Department of the Air Force
Approved for public release; distribution unlimited

PROJECT AIR FORCE

For more information on this publication, visit **www.rand.org/t/RRA1125-1**.

**About RAND**

The RAND Corporation is a research organization that develops solutions to public policy challenges to help make communities throughout the world safer and more secure, healthier and more prosperous. RAND is nonprofit, nonpartisan, and committed to the public interest. To learn more about RAND, visit www.rand.org.

**Research Integrity**

Our mission to help improve policy and decisionmaking through research and analysis is enabled through our core values of quality and objectivity and our unwavering commitment to the highest level of integrity and ethical behavior. To help ensure our research and analysis are rigorous, objective, and nonpartisan, we subject our research publications to a robust and exacting quality-assurance process; avoid both the appearance and reality of financial and other conflicts of interest through staff training, project screening, and a policy of mandatory disclosure; and pursue transparency in our research engagements through our commitment to the open publication of our research findings and recommendations, disclosure of the source of funding of published research, and policies to ensure intellectual independence. For more information, visit www.rand.org/about/research-integrity.

RAND's publications do not necessarily reflect the opinions of its research clients and sponsors.

*Cover: Left, Air Force photo by Master Sgt. Donald R. Allen; Right, Z2A1/Alamy Stock Photo.*

# About This Report

A primary focus of the 2018 U.S. National Defense Strategy is the growing air and missile threat of potential adversaries. As a result, joint force development is focused on solving the operational problem of fighting effectively and winning in increasingly contested environments. This has led to the development of *adaptive basing* (AB) and other concepts that could reduce the vulnerability of U.S. forces while enhancing the warfighting capability through maneuver and other nonstandard approaches. AB and similar concepts call for force packages to operate in mobile and responsive ways to preserve critical U.S. combat capabilities and fight from positions of advantage. Many organizations are developing innovative AB concepts to address these issues. These concepts place demands on the U.S. Air Force's global mobility capabilities, but the effects on the Mobility Air Forces (MAF) have not been fully analyzed.

Air Mobility Command A5/8 (Strategic Plans, Requirements and Programs) asked RAND Project AIR FORCE (PAF) to assess the impact of AB concepts now being developed regarding the demand for MAF assets. This project specifically focuses on the MAF's current ability to support air refueling demand, airlift demand, and base enablers required by AB concepts and ways to enhance that capability. This project is intended to provide the analytical underpinning to help Air Mobility Command leaders move forward with modernization; capability development; implementation of new tactics, techniques, and procedures; and force structure planning decisions to enhance the ability of the MAF to support AB operations. This research should be of interest to personnel involved in adaptive basing operations, air refueling, airlift, logistics, sustainment, and base operations in the U.S. Air Force. The research is discussed in three companion reports:

- *How Can the Mobility Air Forces Better Support Adaptive Basing? Summary Analysis, Findings, and Recommendations*, RR-A1125-1, 2023. **This volume provides essential findings and recommendations for a broad audience, including U.S. Air Force decisionmakers.**
- *How Can the Mobility Air Forces Better Support Adaptive Basing? Appendixes A–C, Supporting Analyses of Adaptive Basing, Soft Power, and Historical Case Studies*, RR-A1125-2, 2023. This volume provides in-depth discussion of the AB concepts being developed, a detailed examination of the different types of power (hard, soft, and sharp) an adversary could exert on potential allies to limit U.S. base access, and historical case studies from World War II. **This volume is intended for military planners and analysts interested in adaptive basing concepts writ large, including political challenges and historical precedents.**
- *How Can the Mobility Air Forces Better Support Adaptive Basing? Appendixes D–I, Supporting Analyses of Tankers, Airlift, and Base Enablers*, forthcoming, Not available to the general public. This volume presents the detailed quantitative analysis underlying

our conclusions. **This volume is intended for the analyst community, as well as those interested in the details, approach, and assumptions of the analysis conducted.**

The research reported here was commissioned by the director of strategic plans, requirements, and programs at Air Mobility Command and conducted within the Strategy and Doctrine Program of RAND Project AIR FORCE as part of a fiscal year 2019 project titled Rapid Global Mobility Support of Adaptive Basing Concepts. The views expressed in this report are those of the authors and do not reflect the official policy or position of the Department of Defense or the U.S. government.

## RAND Project AIR FORCE

RAND Project AIR FORCE (PAF), a division of the RAND Corporation, is the Department of the Air Force's (DAF's) federally funded research and development center for studies and analyses, supporting both the United States Air Force and the United States Space Force. PAF provides the DAF with independent analyses of policy alternatives affecting the development, employment, combat readiness, and support of current and future air, space, and cyber forces. Research is conducted in four programs: Strategy and Doctrine; Force Modernization and Employment; Resource Management; and Workforce, Development, and Health. The research reported here was prepared under contract FA7014-16-D-1000.

Additional information about PAF is available on our website: www.rand.org/paf/

This report documents work originally shared with the DAF in October 2019. The draft report, issued on September 27, 2019, was reviewed by formal peer reviewers and DAF subject-matter experts.

## Acknowledgments

We would first like to thank our project sponsor, Major General Mark Camerer, Air Mobility Command A5/8. General Camerer spent a great deal of time with us providing guidance, insights, and assistance throughout this project. He is a fantastic sponsor of RAND research, generously engaging his analytic and logical mind to guide the work. We would also like to thank his predecessor, Major General John Wood. General Wood made a very strong case for this project's inclusion in the RAND Project Air Force research agenda for fiscal year 2019. General Wood had the initial insight of the importance of this work and convincingly described it to a senior steering group, which resulted in project funding.

At Air Mobility Command, we would first like to thank our action officers, Craig Lundy, and Major Andrea Harrington. We would also like to thank the great analysts in A9, Jim Donovan, Pete Szabo, John O'Neill, and Randy Johnson. Several other Air Mobility Command staff and unit members provided crucial insight and information to support this study. Among them were Lt Col Jeremiah Custillo, Brian Heriford, Maj Sam Dunlap, and Maj Eric McConville. We had the occasion to travel to meet with the Pacific Air Forces staff. Key help came from Maj Kai Grager, Col Matt Daack, and Brigadier General Michael Winkler. Finally, we received support from Col Kevin Hecke at the Air Force Installation and Mission Support Center and Col Brad Johnson at the U.S. Air Force Expeditionary Center.

At RAND, we would first like to thank Paula Thornhill, who provided insightful advice and feedback throughout the project. We would also like to thank Chris Gilmore, who contributed to this project during his time at RAND. Michael Kennedy and Anthony Rosello did an outstanding job reviewing an earlier draft of this report, providing helpful comments and suggestions for improvement. Finally, we would like to express our sincere appreciation to the editors and artists who turned our work into the final product. Rebecca Fowler did a great job editing the report. Julienne Ackerman skillfully guided the report through the publications process. We are grateful to Rick Penn-Kraus for his fantastic work on the cover design.

# Summary

## Issue

The U.S. National Defense Strategy highlighted important new strategic and operational challenges and called on the U.S. Department of Defense to innovate in response to those challenges. The U.S. Air Force is exploring adaptive basing (AB) concepts as part of this innovation to reduce the vulnerability of combat air forces (CAF) and to preserve critical combat capabilities in highly contested environments.[1] These AB concepts will stress the Mobility Air Forces (MAF). Given the uncertainty of the emerging operational environment, enhancing MAF adaptability will create a significant national strategic advantage for the United States.

## Approach

From a broad range of AB options being developed, we identified four concepts to represent a range of challenges to mobility operations. We analyzed the implications of each on the demand for tankers, airlift, and base enablers.[2] These concepts, and the baseline, are illustrated in Figure S.1. We examined the *sufficiency* of current MAF capacity to support the CAF using AB concepts and then considered *potential enhancements* to better support AB operations.

**Figure S.1. Basing Concepts Analyzed**

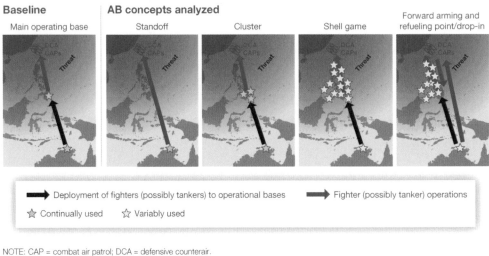

NOTE: CAP = combat air patrol; DCA = defensive counterair.

---

[1] Throughout this report, we use the term *adaptive basing* (AB) to represent a range of concepts in which fighters operate dynamically from forward austere bases. One of these concepts was *agile combat employment* (ACE). Since completion of this work, ACE has become a widely used term for these operations.

[2] We used operations in the Pacific for the analytical cases, but the results should be applicable across different theaters when one considers differences in distances, bases, etc.

## Conclusions

In terms of sufficiency, we find the following:

- Different AB concepts and different implementation approaches have vastly different implications for the MAF.
- Under most circumstances, the MAF could support small elements of CAF fighters (about ten 24-hour, two-ship DCA CAPs) using AB concepts with tankers from standoff—but only by engaging a large fraction of the MAF fleet. There are some cases in which the MAF would have difficulty supporting even this level of combat power.
- MAF units are not sized or structured to support AB concepts: The U.S. Air Force force packaging and equipping strategy is not designed to deploy small packages at large scale.
- Under most circumstances, base enablers (e.g., contingency response forces and base operation support) could support the AB cases analyzed, but an entire theater campaign would stress resources.
- Command-and-control coordination between the CAF and MAF, vulnerability of communications and navigation, and MAF culture offer additional challenges.

Several enhancements could help the MAF to support larger elements of combat power using AB. Our analysis suggests the following:

- Tankers will likely need to operate closer to the fight to meet large AB demands.
- Minimizing forward ground times and operating from multiple forward bases could enhance tanker survivability. Return to standoff bases as required for major maintenance.
- When possible, ground transportation could reduce the intratheater airlift requirement.
- New systems and concepts of operations (CONOPs) could shorten airlift ground times, enhance logistical operations, and cut the deployed footprint.
- Cross-training personnel could reduce deployed footprint, relieve shortfalls, and improve deployment and employment timelines.
- Increasing and expanding contingency response capability and capacity are required to support large theater-wide operations, if using AB.
- Joint, host-nation, contract support, and prepositioning could offset some airlift demand.
- Seeking agreements in advance with potential partners, such as the predesignated bases in the U.S.-Philippines Enhanced Defense Cooperation Agreement, is highly desirable.

## Recommendations for Air Mobility Command

- Enhance integration with the CAF, joint, and component organizations to ensure that AB plans are developed in line with air mobility strengths and constraints.
- Experiment with new CONOPs to allow the MAF to best support AB operations.
- Coordinate with allied governments to enhance the potential for desirable basing and to better mitigate impacts on operations due to Chinese use of hard, soft, or sharp power.
- Conduct a complete review of rules and regulations (e.g., Air Force instructions) to enable more-effective operations in challenging environments while taking prudent risk.

- Consider how new equipment and technologies (discussed in this report) and new CONOPs could enable safer, more-efficient, and more-effective AB operations.

# Contents

# Figures

# Table

# 1. Introduction

The summary of the 2018 National Defense Strategy (NDS) states that potential adversaries are challenging the ability of U.S. forces to maintain access to bases and airspace needed to support joint and combined forces.[1] The NDS summary specifically identifies issues with a potential near-peer adversary in the Pacific: "China is leveraging military modernization, influence operations, and predatory economics to coerce its neighboring countries to reorder the Indo-Pacific region to their advantage."[2] The NDS summary further discusses the growing air and missile threat of potential adversaries and focuses joint force development on solving the operational problem of fighting effectively and winning under these conditions.

History has shown that the United States has successfully sustained air operations while under attack in an improvised, undermanned, and dynamic environment.[3] Many lessons that were learned in the past are applicable today, such as the importance of basing, prepositioning, and nimble operations, as well as the need to enhance overall deployed capability by having personnel cross-trained in multiple specialties. The United States has confronted and overcome many of these same challenges in the past.

For many years, there has been a great deal of work analyzing the effect of antiaccess/area denial or contested, degraded, and operationally limited environments on USAF operations.[4] That analysis focused primarily on the effects of air base attack and potential mitigation options, with the goal of permitting high-tempo operations from these air bases. Analysis has shown that these mitigation approaches—which consist of active defenses, base hardening, deception, and other passive measures, such as dispersal of assets on a base—could have a meaningful and

---

[1] U.S. Department of Defense, *Summary of the 2018 National Defense Strategy of the United States of America, Sharpening the American Military's Competitive Edge*, Washington, D.C., 2018.

[2] U.S. Department of Defense, 2018, p. 1.

[3] Although the U.S. Air Force (USAF) has largely not had to deal with the issue of air base attack since the end of the Cold War, this is not a new problem. In an appendix (David T. Orletsky, Michael Kennedy, Bradley DeBlois, Daniel M. Norton, Richard Mason, Dahlia Anne Goldfeld, Andrew Karode, Jeff Hagen, James S. Chow, James Williams, Alexander C. Hou, and Michael J. Lostumbo, *Options to Enhance Air Mobility in Anti-Access/Area Denial Environments*, Santa Monica, Calif.: RAND Corporation, 2022, Not available to the general public) we present World War II case studies. This historical work showed that the United States adopted several approaches to address this challenge, including a joint approach, specialized forces trained in forward operations, dual-hatted personnel, modifications to equipment and tactics, and flight crews conducting ground tasks.

[4] At the RAND Corporation, much of this work was accomplished under the Combat Operations in Denied Environments (CODE) umbrella of projects. For a discussion of findings and lessons learned from years of CODE work, along with an annotated bibliography of recent CODE reports, see Robert S. Tripp, Alan J. Vick, Jacob L. Heim, and James A. Leftwich, *Increasing Air Base Resilience to Missile Attacks: Lessons Learned from RAND Analyses on Combat Operations in Denied Environments*, Santa Monica, Calif.: RAND Corporation, 2022, Not available to the general public. These projects that are specifically focused on air base attack have been ongoing since 2013 and have been conducted for multiple USAF and joint sponsors.

significant impact on improving aircraft survivability and permitting USAF operations. However, that analysis has also shown that assumptions about the level and capability of the threat and effectiveness of the active and passive defense measures can have big impacts on the results. Further, many of these approaches depend on large infrastructure investments involving base hardening and other measures to increase survivability. These infrastructure investments will often require the identification of particular operational bases well in advance of a conflict. Consistent with these concerns, the NDS summary highlights the need for forward force maneuver and posture resilience: "Investments will prioritize ground, air, sea, and space forces that can deploy, survive, operate, maneuver, and regenerate in all domains while under attack. Transitioning from large, centralized, unhardened infrastructure to smaller, dispersed, resilient, adaptive basing that include active and passive defenses will also be prioritized."[5] As a result, joint force development is focused on solving the operational problem of fighting effectively and winning in increasingly contested environments.

This focus on maneuver has led to the development of *adaptive basing* (AB) and other concepts that could reduce the vulnerability of U.S. forces while enhancing the warfighting capability in contested environments.[6] These concepts primarily involve the dynamic movement of combat air forces (CAF) among multiple bases to complicate adversary targeting. Before AB became a term of art, numerous competing adaptive or dynamic operational concepts emerged. Different organizations throughout the USAF and joint communities have embraced AB and have identified, developed, and begun to experiment with a variety of approaches and concepts, including *flex-basing*, *dynamic basing*, *cluster basing*, *Rapid Raptor*, *Rapid-X*, *untethered operations*, *joint forward area refueling point (FARP)*, and *agile combat employment*.[7]

AB and similar concepts call for force packages to operate in mobile and responsive ways to preserve critical combat capabilities and fight from positions of advantage. AB is gaining support among joint planners as a potential means to address growing tactical challenges. Many organizations, including the warfighting components (e.g., Pacific Air Forces [PACAF] and U.S. Air Forces in Europe [USAFE]) and Air Combat Command, are developing innovative AB concepts.

Although AB concepts are being developed across the CAF, the effect on the Mobility Air Forces (MAF) has not been fully analyzed. AB would place significant demands on USAF's global mobility capabilities, including providing tanker support to the CAF, airlift to rapidly

---

[5] U.S. Department of Defense, 2018, p. 6.

[6] Throughout this report, we use the term *adaptive basing* (AB) to represent a range of concepts in which fighters operate dynamically from forward austere bases. One of these concepts was *agile combat employment* (ACE). Since completion of this work, ACE has become a widely used term for these operations.

[7] See David T. Orletsky, Julia Brackup, Christian Curriden, Adam R. Grissom, Patrick Mills, and Robert A. Guffey, *How Can the Mobility Air Forces Better Support Adaptive Basing? Appendixes A–C, Supporting Analyses of Adaptive Basing, Soft Power, and Historical Case Studies*, Santa Monica, Calif.: RAND Corporation, RR-A1125-2, 2023, Appendix A, for more details on AB concepts.

move personnel and equipment, aerial port capabilities to aid deployment and redeployment, and contingency response forces to help initiate operations at air bases. Air Mobility Command (AMC) A5/8 (Strategic Plans, Requirements and Programs) asked RAND to assess the impact of AB concepts now being developed on the demand for MAF assets.[8] This project assessed the MAF's ability to support the mobility operations required by AB concepts and ways to enhance the capability of the MAF to better support these concepts. It also examined steps that China is taking to use soft, sharp, and hard power to convince and compel U.S. allies in the region to restrict U.S. military access—and China's prospects for success. The reports from this project are intended to provide the analytical underpinning to help AMC leaders move forward with modernization; capability development; implementation of new tactics, techniques, and procedures; and force structure planning decisions to enhance the ability of the MAF to support AB operations.

This report summarizes our analysis and presents the major findings and recommendations. Chapter 2 discuss our analytic approach and briefly outlines the AB concepts that we analyzed. Chapters 3, 4, and 5 present our analysis of tankers, airlifters, and base enablers, respectively. In each case, we analyze the sufficiency of current MAF capabilities to support AB in the Pacific area of operations, then identify potential enhancements to better enable the MAF to support AB operations. Chapter 6 discusses additional issues that AMC should consider as it prepares to meet the AB challenge. Chapter 7 presents our recommendations for AMC.

Separate volumes containing Appendixes A through C and Appendixes D through I provide supporting detail and further information about all the topics covered here, as well as broader discussion of AB and its historical context, the broader dynamics of military access policy in potential host nations, and China's capacity to convince or compel them to deny access for AB.[9] Throughout this report, we note places where the reader can find additional relevant information in those appendixes.

---

[8] Recent RAND work has also shown that in addition to MAF support to joint and combined execution of AB concepts, MAF forces require their own operating and support concepts to become more survivable and responsive. New MAF concepts such as Tanker Continuous Forward Operations have been suggested to better enable the MAF to operate in a contested, degraded, and operationally limited environment. See Orletsky, Kennedy, et al., 2022.

[9] Orletsky, Brackup, et al., 2023; David T. Orletsky, Jeffrey S. Brown, Bradley DeBlois, Patrick Mills, Daniel M. Norton, and Robert A. Guffey, *How Can the Mobility Air Forces Better Support Adaptive Basing? Appendixes D–I, Supporting Analyses of Tankers, Airlift, and Base Enablers*, Santa Monica, Calif.: RAND Corporation, 2023, Not available to the general public.

# 2. Analytic Approach and Selected Adaptive Basing Concepts

This chapter describes the analytical approach and identifies the AB concepts selected for analysis.

## Analytic Approach

The operational problem is how the MAF can best support a range of AB concepts being developed across the USAF. Given that these concepts are still being developed, with considerable variation in approaches,[10] we focused the analysis on four AB concepts that illustrate the challenges these ideas would pose to the MAF. We analyzed MAF operations using each of these broad concepts (plus the current main operating base approach as a baseline) in the Pacific area of responsibility. For each AB concept, we identified the implications for tankers, airlift, and base enablers. In each of these areas, we first considered the sufficiency of current forces to meet the needs of AB concepts in this theater and identified any shortfalls. We then looked for potential ways to eliminate the shortfalls. Drawing from this analysis, we developed findings and recommendations for the MAF to better support AB concepts being developed across the USAF.

## Selection of AB Concepts

AB can make operations more robust by complicating adversary targeting and reducing base density. The disadvantage of AB, from a MAF perspective, is that MAF capabilities will need to respond to contingency requirements that are less predictable and more diverse. Designing the MAF against a static set of specific basing and access assumptions (as is done today) is likely to produce a force that is unable to meet joint requirements in a time of need. Developing a resilient MAF will require dynamism and perhaps inefficiency—attributes that run counter to how the MAF has operated for decades.

Some of the uncertainties in AB are inherent to the concept. Utilizing facilities where the USAF has not operated before and is not based permanently, and which might not be owned by partner central governments, is intrinsically uncertain from a political perspective. In the event of a contingency, the United States may gain access to some of these facilities, be refused others, and receive limited or delayed permission in still others. The overall access picture is likely to be an unpredictable mosaic.

---

[10] Orletsky, Brackup, et al., 2023, describes AB generally and discusses many of the major concepts being considered across the USAF and joint communities.

Other issues associated with AB will be created by adversary efforts to shape the access environment. China, Russia, and similar powers can be expected to take a series of actions to discourage regional states from granting access to the United States, making it increasingly uncertain whether the United States will be granted access to any particular facility, for any particular purpose, during a specific contingency. To play its assigned role in those contingency operations, the MAF must have sufficient capacity and adaptability to cope with the access cards it is dealt on the first day of conflict.[11]

A further source of uncertainty for the MAF today is which of the many AB concepts being proposed (some better defined than others) it may be called on to support. Relative to traditional USAF operations, AB could entail some or all of the following attributes: (1) more locations (i.e., more dispersed), (2) smaller individual deployments, (3) shorter duration deployments, and (4) more flexibility and movement (both operations and support). Thus, the USAF (and AMC specifically) could be supporting numerous, small locations with fairly lean resources, which could come under attack and could require rapid redeployment and response. Not all forces, locations, or phases of a campaign would necessarily operate this way, but *some* forces, *some* locations, and *some* phases could.

All of the above uncertainties collectively make analysis of MAF requirements more challenging. To narrow the range of possibilities, we identified four AB concepts that would present a range of challenges to air mobility. Figure 2.1 illustrates the four concepts and the baseline.

**Figure 2.1. Basing Concepts Analyzed**

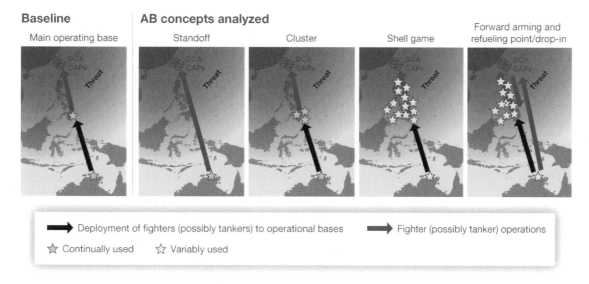

NOTE: CAP = combat air patrol; DCA = defensive counterair.

---

[11] Orletsky, Brackup, et al., 2023, discusses the political challenges to AB and military access in greater detail.

- **Main operating base (baseline):** This is the traditional USAF basing approach, similar to many expeditionary bases already in use, such as Bagram Air Base in Afghanistan.
- **Standoff:** This concept calls for a large, highly capable base with a large number of aircraft operating continuously, but the base is located beyond the range of all but intermediate-range ballistic missiles, resulting in very long fighter and tanker sorties.
- **Cluster basing:** This concept calls for multiple bases, each smaller than a main operating base. Nearby bases share resources via ground lines of communication. We analyzed operations using three and six forward-located cluster bases supporting F-35s.
- **Shell game:** This concept is similar to the cluster concept, except that forces move from base to base over the course of the campaign. Not all bases are flying sorties or are necessarily occupied all the time. In this analysis, we assumed a six-base shell game concept, where one wing of aircraft would operate from any three of the six bases at any time. We evaluated the deployment and employment airlift requirements for different shell game base concepts (e.g., move timelines, initial base operating support [BOS] deployment level to each base, different levels of BOS movement between bases). We assumed a wing of F-35s operating from three of the six bases, where one-third of the wing and 50 percent of the BOS must be moved to the new base each day.[12]
- **FARP/drop-in:** This concept involves two types of bases—a main base that acts as the parent to a number of highly mobile FARP or drop-in bases. Each day, forces at the FARP or drop-in bases move to a (possibly different) forward location, support F-35 operations, and then move back to their parent base. For this work, we investigated concepts using two or four FARP or drop-in bases supported by a single main parent base.

These four concepts (further detailed in this report's companion appendixes) plus the baseline case make up the five concepts we analyze in the Pacific vignette.[13]

## Vignette Assumptions and Variables

We analyzed the five basing concepts in a Pacific vignette.[14] We then considered different force packages and different logistical and sustainment cases. Our force packages consisted of a single fighter wing composed of three 24-aircraft squadrons. This force was sized to support four 24/7 DCA two-ship CAPs.

---

[12] Appendixes F and G (Orletsky, Brown, et al., 2023) show results assuming different levels of BOS movement.

[13] Orletsky, Brackup, et al., 2023.

[14] We used operations in the Pacific in our analysis because they are most demanding. The methodology could be applied to different theaters by applying the relevant distances and base characteristics to the calculations.

This wing was assumed to deploy as part of a larger group of forces in the context of a major conflict. We assumed different mission design series (MDS), including F-35s, F-22s, and F-15C/Ds. Using these force packages, we determined different base logistical and maintenance packages. These variables combined to yield about 60 analytic cases. From that, we then evaluated different types of tankers, airlifters, phases of operation, and concepts of operations (CONOPs). These cases can be found in Appendixes D, E, F, G, and I, in a separate volume.[15] Looking across the cases, we found that the AB concept used has a bigger impact on the MAF support requirement than either fighter type or mission type. Therefore, in the following chapters, we present only the most-relevant cases affecting tankers, airlift, and base enablers, assuming a need to support a wing of F-35As operating in a DCA mission according to the five basing concepts.[16]

All of the AB concepts we examined are vulnerable to attack. We did not look at active and passive defenses, camouflage, concealment and deception, or other options to mitigate the effects of attacks, as they were out of scope. We did examine options for minimizing aircraft time on the ground, which are discussed in the next chapter. Basing concepts in which units move relatively frequently should increase uncertainty in threat targeting and with it the effectiveness of the attacks. Future assessments of AB concepts should examine the threat and alternative mitigation options in more detail.

---

[15] Orletsky, Brown, et al., 2023.

[16] We used F-35s in this analysis because it is a state-of-the art aircraft that is projected to make up the largest fraction of the fighter force by the late 2020s.

# 3. Tanker Support to Adaptive Basing: Current Capability and Potential Enhancements

This chapter estimates the number of tankers required to support 24-hour, two-ship CAPs under each of the five basing concepts identified in Chapter 2, in the context of the Pacific vignette. We analyzed the five basing concepts in multiple ways. For example, the cluster-basing concept indicates that the fighters will operate from bases close to the threat, but we ran cases assuming that tankers operate from the same bases or from standoff locations. We used F-35s in our analysis, since they will make up the majority of the USAF inventory in 2027. In all cases, we assumed that three sets of two F-35s would be required to support two two-ship F-35 CAPs to account for the need to go back to the tanker orbit for fuel while on station. Figure 3.1 shows this graphically in the case of supporting four 24-hour two-ship CAPs. Supporting four CAPs requires that eight F-35s remain on station all of the time. Given the need to go off station for refueling, our calculations are based on the need to have a total of 18 F-35s supporting these four 24-hour CAPs to account for time at the tanker getting refueled, as well as transit time to and from the tanker orbit. Our calculations also include the time and fuel required for both fighters and tankers to transit the distance from base to operating location. From the results, we assessed the sufficiency of the current tanker inventory to meet the demands, then recommended potential enhancements to close any gaps.

**Figure 3.1. Diagram of Tanker and Fighter Operations**

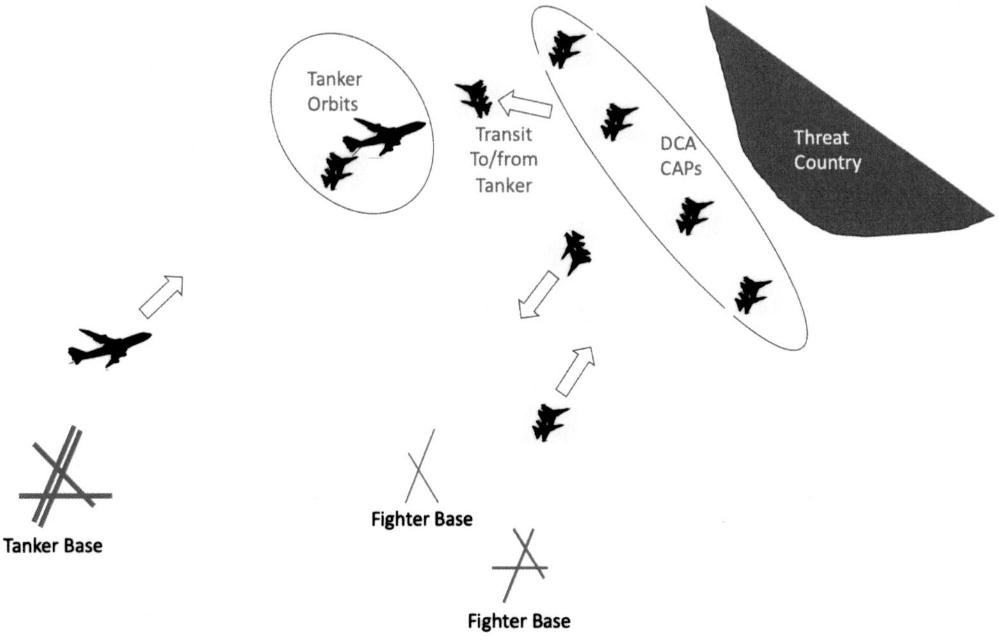

## Sufficiency of Current Tanker Inventory

The current tanker inventory consists of 396 KC-135R/Ts and 59 KC-10As, total active inventory (TAI). USAF is planning for its KC-46 fleet to number 179 KC-46As by 2027. Current plans call for a one-for-one replacement of KC-135s as the new KC-46s are delivered. Drawing on historical experience, we assumed that 85 percent of TAI would be available for operations with the other 15 percent in depot, supporting the schoolhouse, and so on. This results in a combat-coded tanker fleet of 152 KC-46s, 184 KC-135R/Ts, and 50 KC-10As. Since the entire operational fleet of tankers cannot be devoted to a single contingency (e.g., given other worldwide operations and requirements for the nuclear mission), in the Pacific vignette we assume that half of the total available aircraft could be allocated to this scenario: 76 KC-46s, 92 KC-135s, and 25 KC-10s. In addition, we assumed an 85 percent mission capable rate in the calculations.[17]

Looking across the cases we analyzed, the greatest determinant of tanker demand is the standoff distance for both fighters and tankers. Given the number of tankers assumed available to this theater, Figure 3.2 shows the percentage of the tanker capability required to support the fighters in this vignette from different standoff distances.[18] The demand is smallest when both tankers and fighters are close to the operation, as would be true for the baseline basing concept. In this case, the demand is well within the number of tankers we assume would be available for the vignette to support dozens of fighter CAPs. The greatest demand comes from the standoff concept, when both tankers and fighters must operate from long distances (2,000 nm for the fighters and 2,500 nm for the tankers). In this case, the demands exceed the assumed tanker fleet available. The inventory assumed to be available for a conflict in the Pacific for this vignette could support only about nine 24-hour two-ship CAPs. The remaining AB concepts call for fighters to be forward (500 nm in this case), but tankers could operate either forward (1,000 nm) or from standoff (2,500 nm). Thus, the demand would vary between the "tankers and fighters close" and the "tankers standoff, fighters close" lines in Figure 3.2. The latter case could support about a dozen 24-hour two-ship CAPs using the entire tanker fleet available for this scenario.[19]

---

[17] These rates for KC-135 are higher than has been the case recently. Thus, this analysis may understate the number of KC-135s that might be available. See Bradley DeBlois, Thomas Light, Daniel M. Romano, Michael Boito, John G. Drew, Paul Emslie, Michael Kennedy, Kathryn O'Connor, and Jonathan William Welburn, *Options for Enhancing the Effectiveness of Maintenance Force Structure: Examining the Decline in KC-135 Availability*, Santa Monica, Calif.: RAND Corporation, 2020, Not available to the general public.

[18] This analysis assumes that all tankers have sufficient runway and can take off with a maximum fuel load.

[19] The major driver of tanker requirement is degree of standoff for both fighters and tankers. As a result, we present results for tankers and fighters only in terms of standoff distances. See Orletsky, Brackup, et al., 2023, for different AB cases showing equal requirements.

**Figure 3.2. Tanker Demands Across Basing Concepts**

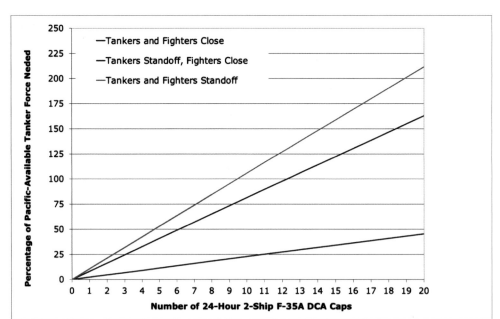

NOTES: The lines on this chart consolidate results for the cases analyzed into "standoff" and "close" categories. A tanker effectiveness equivalency was computed for each tanker type to support CAPs in each of these categories. These equivalencies were then used in combination with the tankers available to compute the percentage of available tanker force needed to support different numbers of CAPs. Results for all cases are presented in Orletsky, Brown, et al., 2023.

The above analysis indicates that, even when there is sufficient inventory to refuel stand-in fighters from standoff range, a very large commitment of tankers is needed to support a modest amount of combat power. Depending on the AB option chosen, tankers from standoff could support nine to 12 CAPs—roughly a little more than half of the fighter force deployed to an Operation Iraqi Freedom–sized operation or about a quarter of the fighters deployed to Operation Desert Storm. Figure 3.3 amplifies this point by showing tanker demand as a function of the fuel offload required, assuming that tankers are supporting operations from 2,500 nm. The red line indicates the offload for four DCA CAPs operating at 500 nm, corresponding to the "tankers standoff, fighters close" lines of Figure 3.2. Increasing the offload requirement to support more fighters would greatly exceed the tanker inventory available for this vignette.

**Figure 3.3. Number of Tankers Required to Support Refueling Operations from Standoff (2,500 nm)**

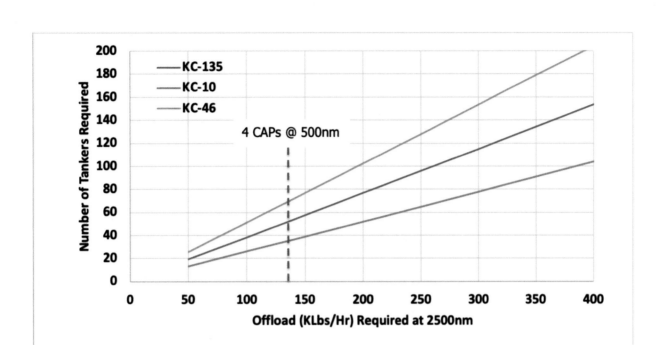

## Potential Enhancements

There are two main approaches to better matching tanker inventory to the requirements of AB concepts. The first is to reduce the demand for tankers when they operate from standoff. The second is to address the two major obstacles preventing tankers from operating closer to the fight: the difficulty of operating from small bases with short runways and the greater exposure to adversary missile threats. We explore several ways to accomplish these aims below.

### Reducing Demand for Standoff Tankers

Operating tankers from standoff range enhances survivability in a contested environment. However, as shown above, the number of tankers required to support nine to 12 DCA CAPs (whether operating from standoff or close to the target area) is at or above the limit of expected tanker inventory. Two enhancements could potentially reduce this demand: force extension and use of a larger "super tanker."[20]

---

[20] On force extension, see Joint Publication 3-17, *Air Mobility Operations*, Washington, D.C.: Joint Chiefs of Staff, February 5, 2019, p. vi-1, for discussion of tanker force extension.

## Force Extension

The KC-10 and the KC-46 are equipped with a receptacle permitting the onloading of fuel from other boom-equipped tankers.[21] Thus, some tankers could offload gas to others during the transit flight to the operational area. Tankers that offloaded the gas could return to base, while the other tankers could go forward with larger fuel loads. This buddy-tanking concept would reduce the number of tankers that have to fly all the way to the refueling area, allowing an increase in the overall tanker fleet sortie rate and reducing the number of tankers required.

Figure 3.4 shows the potential benefit of force extension from standoff distances using KC-46s.[22] In this case, we assume that KC-46s offload fuel to other KC-46s at 1,000 nm before returning to base.[23] The dashed line shows that force extension can reduce the overall tanker demand from standoff locations by up to 25 percent (compared with the solid line). The overall tanker demand would still be much higher than the case in which both tankers and fighters operate from close-in bases (dotted line).

**Figure 3.4. Number of KC-46s Required to Support Refueling Operations from Standoff (2,500 nm), with Buddy Tanking at 1,000 nm**

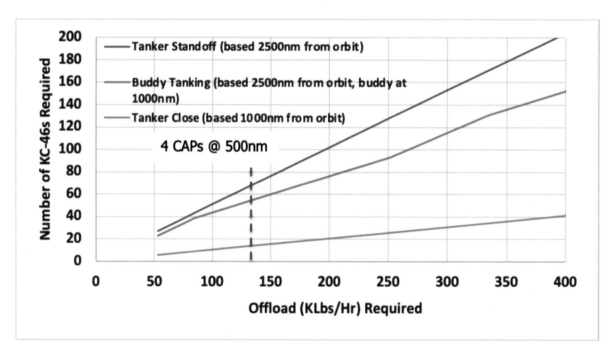

---

[21] Twenty KC-135s also have this capability.

[22] There are many factors driving the efficiency improvement of buddy tanking, including where the offload occurs (distance between base and operating area), types of tankers involved, overall fuel offload required in the operational area, and spikiness (versus steady state) of offload requirement in the operational area. Orletsky, Brown, et al., 2023, shows results for a wide range of cases.

[23] The distance at which buddy tanking takes place could be optimized. The 1,000 nm assumed in Figure 3.4 approximates what could reasonably be expected.

Super Tanker

A more far-term proposal to reduce demand for tankers operating at standoff is to develop a larger tanker. The benefits of a larger tanker are already seen above, where far fewer KC-10s are required than KC-46s or KC-135s. As shown in Figure 3.5, a KC variant with 1.3-million-pound takeoff weight and blended-wing body design[24] operating from standoff could cut the requirement in this vignette by a factor of four or five relative to the number of KC-135s or KC-46s required. This could potentially make it easier for the MAF to support AB operations from the greater safety of standoff range.

**Figure 3.5. Super Tankers Required to Support Refueling Operations from Standoff (2,500 nm)**

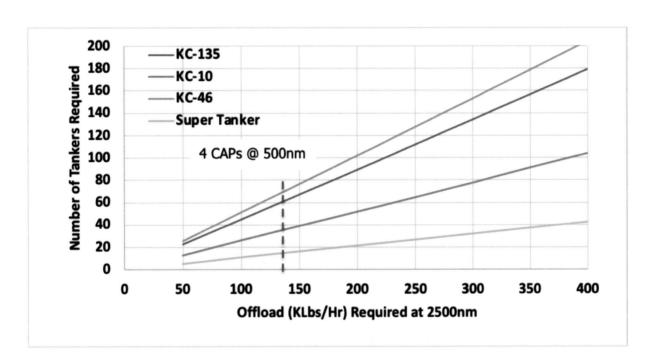

*Reducing Obstacles to Close-in Tanking*

As shown in Figure 3.2, the greatest factor in lowering demand for tankers is the ability to operate both fighters and tankers close to the target area. To take advantage of this benefit, the MAF would need to surmount two major obstacles: the potential need to operate from small bases with shorter runways and a greater exposure to threat.

---

[24] The tanker we used in this analysis is a 1.3-million-pound takeoff-weight tanker design we received from the Air Systems division at Wright-Patterson Air Force Base around 2005. This is a blended wing-body tanker and was provided to RAND as an alternative in the USAF KC-135R recapitalization project conducted during that time frame. We thank David Hammond for providing this design.

Short Runway Tanker Operations

Operating from close-in bases could require the use of smaller bases with shorter runways. In such cases, tanker takeoff fuel load may need to be reduced. Figure 3.6 shows the tanker fuel offload at mission radius for USAF tankers operating from a 9,000-foot runway versus a 12,000-foot runway, assuming a *standard day* or International Standard Atmosphere (ISA).[25] The KC-46 can maintain offload capability from shorter runways better than the legacy tankers. The offload of KC-135 and KC-10 is reduced by 15 percent to 20 percent, while the KC-46 is able to maintain nearly its full capability from 9,000-foot runways.[26] Nevertheless, even with shorter runways, the KC-10 can still deliver more fuel at range than the KC-46. The operational demands of each scenario will determine which tanker fleets are most appropriate to meet the demand. For smaller operations, it might be better to use the KC-10. For larger operations that demand a sizable portion of the tanker fleet to operate from a variety of airfields, the KC-46s may be the most efficient option. It is difficult to see the KC-46 and KC-135 unconstrained offloads on this chart, since these lines are bunched with the "KC-46 (9kft)" line.

**Figure 3.6. Offload at Mission Radius, 12,000-Foot Versus 9,000-Foot Runway, Standard Day (ISA)**

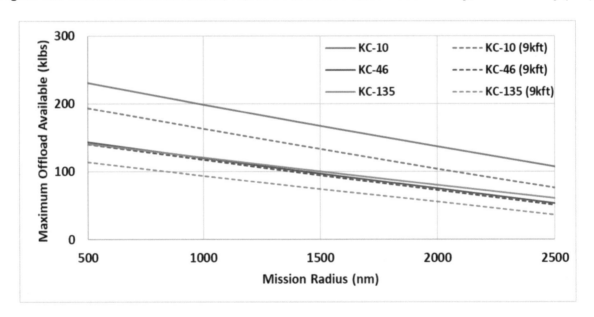

---

[25] Standard day or ISA provides representative conditions on which to conduct aerodynamic calculations and analysis identifying the temperature and pressure conditions. *Standard day* is defined as 59 degrees Fahrenheit (15 degrees Celsius).

[26] We used a 9,000-foot runway for this example because that is where the KC-46 maintains the ability to operate at maximum take-off weight, while the legacy aircraft are forced to operate at lower weights. For all calculations, we used critical field length to determine aircraft weight restrictions at takeoff.

## Minimizing Time-on-Ground

Perhaps the most important issue of operating from closer bases is the potential threat and risk to tankers from ballistic and cruise missile attack. Due to the proliferation of short-range weapons, the threat is typically greater at air bases closer to the adversary than at standoff distances. Many factors go into determining the risk to tankers operating at bases within the threat ring of ballistic and cruise missions, but one of the more important is the amount of time the tankers spend on the ground.

Obviously, an important way to reduce the risk to aircraft on the ground is to keep them flying. There are two considerations here. The first possibility is to operate within the adversary's ability to detect an aircraft on the ground, target the aircraft, and deliver the weapon. This is highly dependent on many factors, including the adversary's sensor and command and control (C2) capability and the defender's capability for camouflage, concealment, and deception.

The second possibility is to simply keep overall ground time in the threat area to a minimum across the entire conflict. One way to accomplish this would be to operate aircraft in theater at a very high utilization (UTE) rate.[27] Figure 3.7 shows how the total ground time is reduced as the UTE rate is increased. Figure 3.2 shows that about 15 tankers were required to support three 24-hour two-ship F-35A DCA CAPs at bases 500 nm from the target area. Assuming a 12-hour tanker UTE rate, this corresponds to 180 total tanker hours on the ground per day in the threat ring—the leftmost point on Figure 3.7. Figure 3.7 shows the "virtuous cycle" of increasing the UTE rate for the tankers in theater. As individual tankers return to the air faster, they spend less time on the ground and are able to fly more sorties per day. Further, since the total tanker requirement equates to total tanker flying hours, increasing the UTE rate of tankers in the threat ring also results in the need for fewer tankers. Therefore, as shown in the figure, increasing the UTE rate by 50 percent (from 12 hours to 18 hours) reduces the total ground hours and exposure to missile and other attacks while there by a factor of three (from 180 to 60 hours per day).

---

[27] One possibility is to embrace a concept that RAND suggested for a fiscal year 2017 project called Tanker Continuous Forward Operations. See Orletsky, Kennedy, et al., 2022. In this concept, a portion of the fleet (say two-thirds) is pushed forward and operated at a very high UTE rate, keeping ground time to an absolute minimum and deferring as much maintenance as possible. When aircraft break, they return to a rear sanctuary base and are replaced with an aircraft that is completely caught up on maintenance and ready to take its turn in theater operating at a very high UTE rate.

**Figure 3.7. Reduction in Total Tanker Ground Time Resulting from Increased Fleet UTE Rate**

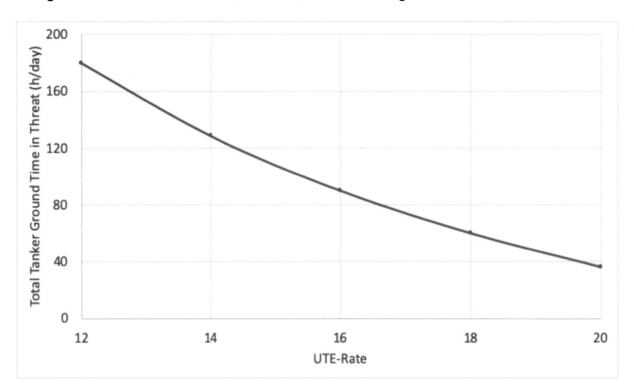

Of course, over time, high UTE rates normally degrade fleet availability. Maintenance cannot keep up with the pace of operations, as aircraft skip normal maintenance actions and begin to break more often. This must be balanced by the safety and maintenance concerns. Notwithstanding this fact, we found that increasing the tanker UTE rate and keeping ground time to an absolute minimum can enhance ground survivability. The reduction in threat to the tanker aircraft on the ground depends on the number of air bases, number of adversary weapons, adversary targeting capability and doctrine, and other factors, but it is clear that reducing total ground time by a significant amount is likely to increase tanker survivability, thereby making close-in basing a more viable option in a contested environment.

## Conclusions

AB concepts could pose significant challenges for the tanker fleet. As currently configured, the MAF could support small numbers of CAF fighters from standoff, but only by leveraging a large fraction of the tanker fleet. Such concepts as buddy tanking or such future capabilities as larger tankers could make it easier to support AB concepts from standoff ranges but do not adequately solve the problem of excessive tanker requirements to support more than a few fighter wings of combat power. Alternatively, the MAF could operate from close-in basing by accepting greater risk and devising CONOPs to mitigate that risk by taking steps to reduce the time that tankers spend on the ground at close-in bases. This appears to be the only near-term solution. USAF should conduct experiments and exercises to better understand the benefits, challenges, costs, and risks of implementing these measures.

# 4. Airlift Support to Adaptive Basing: Current Capability and Potential Enhancements

Similar to tankers, airlift will likely face increased demand when supporting CAF in the context of AB. Airlifters will need to deploy resources to a larger number of operating locations and sustain forces during the conflict, including the movement of resources among bases in the case of the shell game and FARP/drop-in concepts.

To estimate the potential demand, we analyzed the number of airlifters required to support a wing of fighters flying three 24-hour, four-ship CAPs using four basing concepts (excluding the standoff case) in the Pacific vignette. We examined F-22s, F-15s, and F-35s in both air-to-air and strike roles. Similar to the tanker analysis, we found that the results were relatively insensitive to the type of fighter and type of mission. In this chapter we present results from using F-35As in an air-to-air combat role to support their DCA mission described in previous chapters.[28] We first estimate the sufficiency of current airlift fleets to support demand under each AB concept, then review potential enhancements to reduce shortfalls.

## Sufficiency of Current Airlift Inventory

According to Air Force Pamphlet 10-1403, the MAF has 254 C-130s (110 C-130Js mostly in the active duty and 144 C-130Hs mostly in the Air National Guard and Air Force Reserve), 48 C-5Ms, and 188 C-17s.[29] We assumed that 35 percent of each of these fleets could be available for use supporting a wing of F-35s conducting AB operations in the Pacific. We estimate this to be a reasonable maximum, given the priority such a conflict would likely have balanced against all the other service and joint requirements outside F-35s. This leaves us with available fleet sizes of 89 C-130s, 17 C-5Ms, and 66 C-17s for the Pacific vignettes examined here.[30]

### *Deployment Demand*

Figure 4.1 shows the number of C-17s or C-130s required to deploy the fighter package from a standoff base in theater approximately 1.300 nm to their forward basing locations in a five-day

---

[28] Results for all cases are given in Orletsky, Brown, et al., 2023.

[29] Air Force Pamphlet 10-1403, *Air Mobility Planning Factors*, Washington, D.C.: U.S. Department of the Air Force, October 24, 2018.

[30] Appendix E (Orletsky, Brown, et al., 2023) shows results for C-5Ms. We do not include them in the remainder of this chapter because they are less likely to be used in this vignette than C-130s or C-17s. We do not show C-5Ms in Figure 4.1, since these aircraft are not as well suited for operations on the smaller, less capable airfields that are anticipated during AB operations. Further, a demand intertheater (strategic) airlift will also likely exist, and the C-5Ms are more likely to be devoted to this operation.

window. The airlift demand for any AB concept can vary depending on the existence of a forward base, the availability of prepositioned materiel, or host-nation support. The chart therefore shows two demand cases: one in which everything needed must be airlifted (most stressing) and another in which the operation can "fall in" on existing forward bases (least stressing).[31]

**Figure 4.1. Airlift Fleet Size Required to *Deploy* Different AB Concepts**

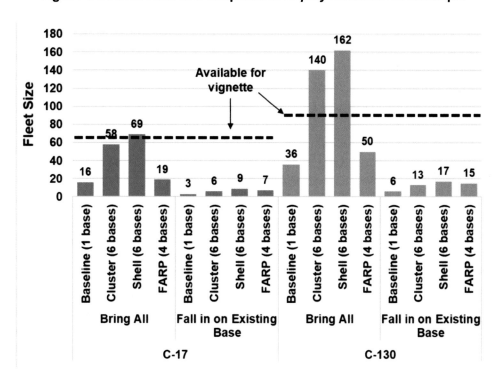

When comparing Figure 4.1 with our expected number of operational aircraft devoted to this contingency, we see that deploying a single wing of fighter aircraft can require a significant amount of airlift. In the case of the Shell-6 concept, C-17s would require seven C-130s to augment to deploy the wing, depending on assumptions about the availability of equipment and resources in place (including host nation and prepositioning). This contrasts with the much-reduced airlift need when host nation support or prepositioning is available. As a result, certain AB concepts using more than a three 24 primary aircraft authorized (PAA) F-35 squadrons would stress the available airlift, unless a large deployment time window exists or host-nation support or prepositioned equipment is available to reduce the total airlift burden.

---

[31] Orletsky, Brown, et al., 2023, shows results for intermediate cases. That report also assesses a range of options to reduce the footprint and therefore airlift demand, including increased reliance on host-nation capabilities, USAF prepositioned equipment stocks, and joint or contract support.

*Sustainment Demand*

Figure 4.2 shows the fleet size of C-17s or C-130s required to sustain or employ the deployed fighter package from a standoff base in theater approximately 1,300 nm from their forward basing locations. In addition to standard planning factors for the number of people, we assumed a 100 percent use rate per fighter sortie for munitions, one load of fuel for each fighter sortie in the FARP/drop-in cases (fuel was assumed to be available for other basing concepts), and fighter spare parts using standard logistic planning factors. Significantly, the results for shell game and FARP/drop-in basing concepts include movement of resources among bases. In the shell game case, the analysis modeled the movement of 50 percent of one shell base per day. In the FARP/drop-in concept, four FARPs move from a standoff main base *twice* each day: eight hours to move and set up, eight hours to operate, and eight hours to return.

As expected, the shell game and FARP/drop-in concepts require more airlift to sustain than traditional concepts, as they include the redeployment of "bases" each day within the theater. In these cases, about one-third to one-half of the available C-17 fleet or one-half to most of the expected C-130 fleet could be required to support three 24/7 DCA CAPs. The FARP/drop-in cases are the same regardless of the infrastructure deployment case examined (bringing everything versus falling in), since we assumed that these are very short-duration locations with minimal or no maintenance capability. In both cases, all required items to refuel and rearm the aircraft are brought in during the employment operation.

**Figure 4.2. Airlift Fleet Size Required to *Employ* Different AB Concepts**

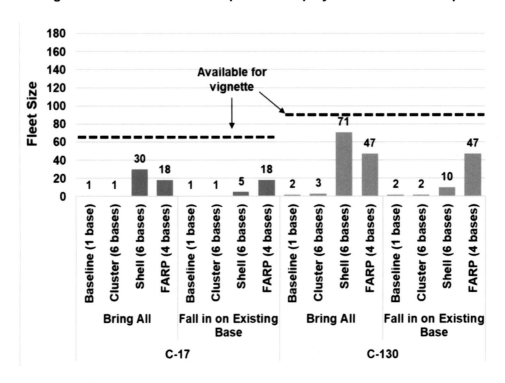

We find the airlift requirement to support AB concepts is feasible but can require nearly the entire expected airlift fleet to deploy the force, depending on which concept is employed and how much support must be airlifted in. Employment demands are more modest. The use of prepositioned or host-nation support is advisable to reduce the demand on MAF airlifters.

## Potential Enhancements

Like tankers, airlifters will be doubly challenged in a contested environment: They must keep up with the higher demands levied by AB concepts, and they must spend time at bases that will likely be targeted by the adversary. We consider several potential approaches to addressing these issues below.

### Using Ground Transportation to Reduce Airlift Demand

The two most stressing AB concepts for airlift involve the movement of resources among bases. Use of ground transportation could help alleviate this demand. To illustrate, we assessed how many airlifters could be saved by diverting some of the movements to trucks, using notional base locations and road networks on the island of Mindanao in the Philippines.[32] We examined the ability of U.S. Army truck companies with 40 M1075A1 Palletized Load System (PLS) trucks and 40 M1083A1 medium tactical vehicle (MTV) trucks to reduce the need for airlift. We assumed that the truck companies were prepositioned on the island and that Army personnel were flown in to operate them prior to the start of operations.[33] We also modeled the demand for airlifters in the same cases. For simplicity, we present the results only for the C-17 below.[34] Next, we present the effect of using trucks for both the shell game and FARP/drop-in concepts.

#### With Shell Game Concept

As we saw in the airlift analysis, the movement of shell bases puts large demands on the airlift fleet. In this section, we assess new ways to move the units to reduce airlift demand. In the aircraft analysis, we based the airlifters at a main base far from the threat. Here, we base the airlifters on the same island as the fighters, vary the share of the fighter squadrons moved, and use Army trucks in place of airlifters to move those squadrons. We combined the six bases in the shell game into three pairs according to proximity, as shown in Figure 4.3. We modeled the movement of one squadron within a 24-hour window, with every squadron moving every three

---

[32] The analysis of road networks is given in Orletsky, Brown, et al., 2023. We did not do a quantitative analysis of how sealift would affect demand in this vignette; however, we expect that sealift could reduce the need for airlift, depending on situational variables, such as the additional time needed to load and unload the ships and the location of the ports relative to the air bases.

[33] We assessed the contribution of the Army Transportation Composite Truck Company (Light). These are found in the active and reserve components. Other Army and Marine Corps transportation companies, or host-nation or commercial transportation, could also be used.

[34] Orletsky, Brown, et al., 2023, presents results for C-130s and C-5s.

days. Each squadron shuttles back and forth between the bases in its base pair, with each base occupied half of the time. We modeled two cases, one in which 50 percent of the equipment and personnel on a shell base moved and one in which 75 percent moved.

**Figure 4.3. Philippine Bases and Routes**

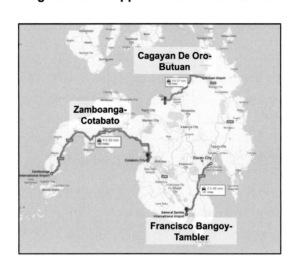

Figure 4.4 shows the number of airlifters or trucks needed for the 50 percent and 75 percent shell base movement cases. In both cases, vehicles that could self-deploy did so.[35] In the 50 percent case, 1.5 truck companies could eliminate the need for 14 C-17s. In the second, 2.3 truck companies could eliminate the need for 21 C-17s. The use of Army truck companies could also eliminate working maximum on ground (WMOG) requirements, which range from 4.9 to 7.4 C-17 equivalents using standard planning assumptions. Many of the small bases envisioned for these types of operations will not support this level of aircraft MOG.

---

[35] These vehicles were composed of light, medium, and heavy trucks. In this assessment, we moved the same amount of personnel, equipment, and supplies as in the previous section. With the same inputs, we would get the same estimate of demand for C-17s (30) for the "bring everything" shell (six bases) case shown in Figure 4.2. There were only two differences. First, trucks that could be driven from one base to another within the movement timeline were moved that way to limit airlift demands. This reduced the need for airlift by about 18 percent. Second, as the airlifters were flying from one location on the island to another, their travel times were much shorter than those in the previous case, in which units deployed from a standoff base 2,500 nm away. As a result, airlift sortie rates were four per day, or more than twice that of the previous case. Together, these changes reduced the number of aircraft needed by 60 percent.

**Figure 4.4. Comparison of Airlift Versus Truck Company Employment for Shell Game Basing**

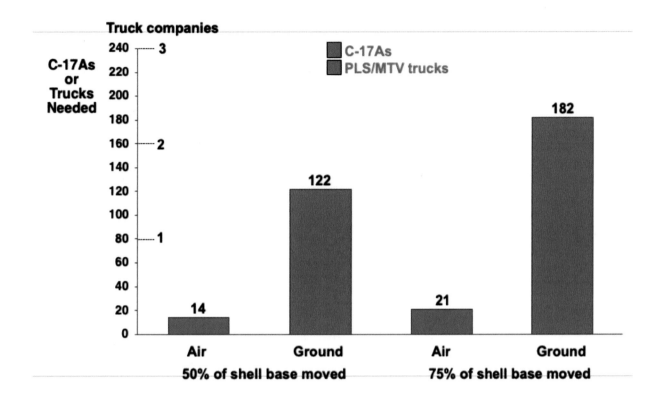

## With FARP/Drop-in Concept

In the FARP/drop-in case, we assumed that aircraft deployed from a single main operating base, Francisco Bangoy International, to two or four FARP or drop-in locations. The movement window was eight hours. We assumed that all equipment and supplies could be prepared for movement and palletized prior to the 2.75-hour load time. We similarly assumed that they could be depalletized and readied for use during the 2.75-hour unload time. All of the air and surface lift options are viable for all routes under these assumptions.

In that case, 1.2 to 1.6 companies could replace the need for 13 to 16 C-17s while eliminating the need for MOG.[36] Replacing C-17s with Army trucks is feasible only when suitable roads are available.[37] Figure 4.5 shows the results for the FARP/drop-in cases. Given the high level of payoff, this should be considered if the timeline issues can be resolved.

---

[36] In Figure 4.2, we showed a demand for 18 C-17s to support fighter operations at four FARPs. In this case, 13 percent of the force could self-deploy via the road network, reducing the number of aircraft needed to 16. In this case, the aircraft sortie rate would be the same, due to the short deployment window.

[37] The road network was sufficient in every region we examined.

**Figure 4.5. Comparison of Airlift Versus Truck Company Employment for FARP or Drop-in Basing**

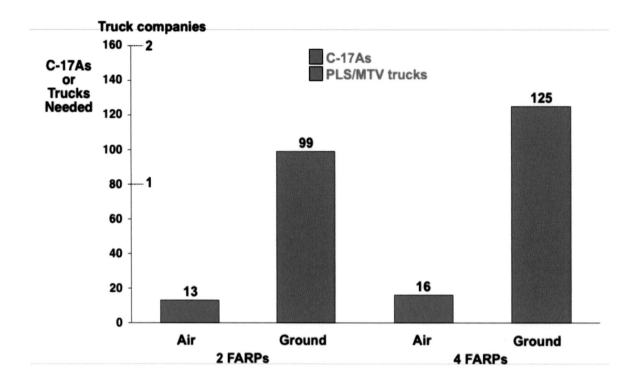

### Extending C-130J-30 Capability

The majority of the C-130Js in the USAF inventory are C-130J-30s (the stretch version with eight pallet positions) with no external fuel tanks. The C-130J-30 has a normal maximum gross weight of 164,000 lb, which can be waived to 175,000 lb. We analyzed whether waiving the maximum weight to 175,000 lb and installing external fuel tanks could reduce the number required to support AB concepts (see Figure 4.6). By measuring in tons moved per 24 hours per individual tail, we found that the benefit of putting external fuel tanks on C-130J-30 aircraft is a four-way balance between the weight and drag penalty of the tanks versus the time saved by not stopping or diverting for fuel versus the additional payload gained by stopping versus the risk of landing in a threat environment. In the scenarios analyzed, we found no gain in adding external fuel tanks to a C-130J-30 unless maximum gross weight is also waived to 175,000 lb. If landing is *not* possible or desirable, then a C-130J-30ER (with externals) waived to a maximum gross weight of 175,000 lb will outperform a slick wing C-130J-30 also waived to 175,000 at all distances beyond 2,000 nm. Short of that distance, the slick wing aircraft has the advantage. If a fuel stop *is* possible, the advantage of having external fuel tanks narrows to a distance band between 2,000 nm and at most 2,500 nm. Short of 2,000 nm, the slick wing variant can carry more cargo, and fly faster, than the external-tank version. Beyond 2,500 nm, it is better to stop for fuel since the additional cargo weight the aircraft can then carry more than makes up for the cycle-time penalty incurred by stopping. We look at the impact of shorter-range vignettes in the appendixes.[38]

**Figure 4.6. Comparison of C-130J Fleet Sizes to Employ a Four-Base FARP/Drop-in Concept**

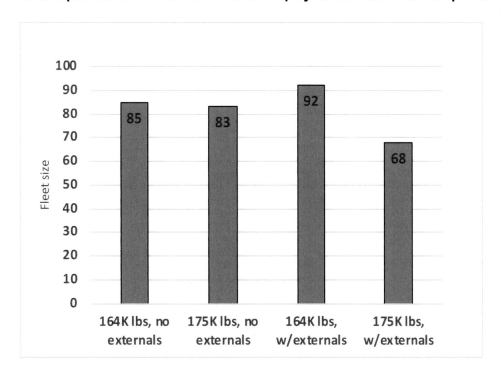

*Reducing Time on the Ground*

As in the tanker analysis, we considered various ways to reduce the time airlifters spend on the ground, both to increase survivability and potentially to reduce fleetwide demand in this vignette. We identified six ways to reduce airlift time on the ground:

1. **Expedited offload:** Expedited ground times (as presented in Air Force Pamphlet 10-1403) include either onload or offload, without refueling or reconfiguring.[39] Although typically not done in peacetime, concurrent fueling and cargo operations should allow airlifters to both refuel (if available) and either onload or offload within an expedited ground time.
2. **Engine running offload:** This is a commonly used procedure by MAF airlifters to expedite ground times. Using this method, the aircraft is offloaded with its engines running, which shortens ground time by eliminating the time required to do postflight, preflight, and engine starting checklists and procedures. We did not refuel aircraft at the offload base when using engine running offload procedures.
3. **Roll-off trucks and trailers:** Further time savings and flexibility could be realized through the use of roll-off trucks towing trailers, each loaded with munitions, supplies,

---

[38] See Orletsky, Brown, et al., 2023.

[39] Air Force Pamphlet 10-1403, 2018.

and fuel and fuel bladders (where appropriate). Trucks and trailers loaded with cargo could be driven off at the destination location, then empty trucks or trailers from previous sorties would be driven on the aircraft for retrograde. Some of this could be accommodated by current vehicles in the USAF inventory; some might be better suited to designing or retrofitting a truck to carry equipment and supplies that are normally palletized. The two disadvantages to this are, first, the expense of using trucks and trailers when pallets were previously used and, second, that because those vehicles are so heavy and bulky by themselves, the process would probably cut in half the net carrying capacity of most airlifters. This strategy could be suitable for certain classes or categories of equipment.

4. **Combat offload:** This method of airland delivery is somewhat like an airdrop on the ground. It involves taxiing the aircraft out from underneath a palletized load, which moves on rollers out behind the aircraft.

5. **Wheeled pallet (nonmotorized or remote-controlled "robo-pallet"):** These technologies would enable some types of palletized cargo to be offloaded (or onloaded) without the use of forklifts or other material handling equipment.[40]

6. **Airdrop:** In this case, cargo is rigged with parachutes and dropped to the supporting base.

Table 4.1 shows our assumptions of ground time for the different approaches considered. We started with USAF planning factors and modified according to our judgment to analyze the cases outlined above.

**Table 4.1. Airlifter Ground Times for Cases Examined**

| Ground Time (hrs) | C-17ER | C-130J-30 |
|---|---|---|
| Normal | 2.75 | 2 |
| Expedited | 2.25 | 1.75 |
| Engine Running Offload (ERO) | 1.00 | 0.75 |
| Combat Offload / Roll-Off | 0.5 | 0.4 |
| Airdrop | 0 | 0 |

Any reduction in ground time could make airlifters more survivable in contested environments. As discussed in Chapter 5, some of the time-saving measures presented in this section would also have benefits in terms of base enabling capabilities. However, each measure has drawbacks that should be considered. Notably, the vignette analysis found that that reducing ground time does not appreciably lower the demand for airlifters to support AB concepts.[41]

---

[40] There are, of course, even more-sophisticated automated or robotic material handling technologies, but the motivation here is to find something inexpensive, simple, and flexible enough to be well suited to the timelines and environments of AB operations.

[41] Orletsky, Brown, et al., 2023, discusses advantages and drawbacks of these time-saving methods in greater detail. It also details the impact of ground time-saving measures on airlift demand in this vignette.

## Conclusions

The virtue of AB concepts lies in their ability to confuse the adversary by multiplying the number of bases where the CAF might operate and, in some cases, moving operations among bases during the conflict. These attributes will place greater burdens on airlifters, both to deploy and to sustain forces. Not all AB concepts analyzed have the same impact; cluster basing and shell game concepts place the greatest demands for airlift to deploy and sustain forces, and the FARP/drop-in concept places heavy demands during the employment phase. The C-17 fleet is better able to meet these demands than the C-130 fleet. But as with tankers, a large number of MAF forces is required to support a small amount of combat power. USAF should explore ways to reduce demand by (1) enhancing and expanding host-nation support and prepositioning operations, (2) working with other services or host nations to explore the use of ground and sea transportation, and (3) enhancing C-130 capability. (In the next chapter, we discuss further recommendations to work with the CAF to find more appropriate ways to structure force packages.) Given the importance of trade with China to most states in the region and the People's Liberation Army's ability to punish America's regional allies, securing access to host nation facilities and support could prove difficult, requiring close coordination with allies and partners and contingency plans if access is denied in a particular country or region. USAF should also experiment with concepts to reduce the amount of time airlifters must spend on the ground and under threat. USAF should conduct experiments and exercises to better understand the benefits, challenges, costs, and risks of implementing these measures.

# 5. Base Enablers to Support Adaptive Basing: Current Capability and Potential Enhancements

In addition to tankers and airlifters, USAF should consider the impact that AB concepts will have on a broad class of *base enablers*, which includes aircraft maintenance, contingency response (CR) forces, and BOS. This chapter discusses the challenges that AB operations will pose for current base enablers and potential steps to enhance capability.

## Sufficiency

### Aircraft Maintenance

Across the USAF, including the MAF, aircraft maintenance units are sized to support the operational units they are stationed with. They have a parallel force package and unit type code (UTC) design to enable smaller or larger deployment packages to fit the operational need. Typically, these are based on squadron-sized deployments, such that each squadron can operate more or less independently, with flight-line sortie generation and more-intensive on-aircraft and component repair in one geographically collocated unit. But many AB concepts call for forces to decouple sortie generation from repair capabilities and to operate in extremely dispersed packages, sometimes for short durations. MAF units, like most of USAF, are not sized or structured to deploy in small packages at scale.

Irrespective of the total number of aircraft in the entire deployment, each unit (i.e., the sum of its personnel, equipment, and spares) can only split so far. For example, KC-135 and C-130 units with sizes of 12 or 16 PAA and traditional structures could probably split into six- or eight-PAA packages and deploy to two locations instead of one. Dividing personnel and equipment would present the fewest challenges; spare parts would likely be the limiting factor.[42] If highly dispersed packages were required for stand-in cases, either those forward deployments would face challenges in sustaining operations (e.g., constrained spare parts would limit sortie rates) or they would have to "rob" resources from nondeployed units to underwrite their dispersed footprint.[43] It is outside the scope of this analysis to estimate the full tradespace between highly

---

[42] Discussion with 100th Operations Group and 100th Maintenance Group on August 27, 2018, and 317th Airlift Wing on August 21, 2019. Orletsky, Brown et al., 2023, discusses the structure of maintenance units and UTCs in more detail.

[43] It is possible to pool scarce resources, such as spares, within an interdependent network of forward bases, but that solution then creates a demand for transportation across those bases to shunt resources to where they are needed. That need for intratheater (or intranetwork) transportation could be manageable but creates its own challenges, especially in a high-threat environment.

dispersed, forward-deployed forces and the impact of "giving" home-station units for the current force. A clearer theater-wide demand signal for forward dispersal and other basing needs would help determine how far the MAF needs to go to support AB concepts. However, it is worth emphasizing that the KC-135 fleet, at least, already struggles with unit readiness, with contributing causes including maintenance manpower and spares.[44] Dividing that fleet's resources would undoubtedly degrade performance. Below, we recommend some parameters around which UTC force packages could be redesigned.

### CR Force

AB concepts call for the MAF to quickly open and establish several *forward* operating locations.[45] The current en route support system provides some theater-wide throughput capacity, but its capacity is limited, it would likely be devoted to large-scale deployment in a major contingency, and its locations are a means to get to forward locations. Traditional aerial port squadrons have deployable units, but those units do not have the speed or breadth of competencies required to support AB concepts. However, CR forces are uniquely suited to provide the required speed and capability.[46] We therefore examined whether current CR forces have the capability to provide responsive forward support to AB concepts in the Pacific vignette.

One way to measure this capability is the WMOG, or the maximum number of aircraft that can be simultaneously serviced on the ground with the intent to relaunch the plane as soon as possible.[47] We estimate the WMOG needs for AB concepts but do not assess the overall sufficiency of the entire global or theater en route support structure to support the deployment of an entire time-phased force deployment data or campaign-sized force.

Our airlift model estimates the WMOG need at each base in our beddown for several aircraft types.[48] Because smaller cargo aircraft (e.g., C-130, as compared with a C-17) have a smaller carrying capacity, more of them are needed in theater and at a given base at one time to meet the deployment or employment demands, relative to larger cargo aircraft. Thus, the WMOG demand

---

[44] A RAND report addressed wartime surge capacity and included a KC-135 case (Patrick Mills, Caolionn O'Connell, Kristin F. Lynch, John G. Drew, Louis W. Miller, Kristin Van Abel, Peter Buryk, Carter C. Price, and Paul Emslie, *Analysis of U.S. Air Force Surge Capacity for Aircraft Availability, Costs, Challenges, and Opportunities*, Santa Monica, Calif.: RAND Corporation, 2017, Not available to the general public). DeBlois et al., 2020, addressed KC-135 maintainer effectiveness.

[45] Note that the rearward or *sending* bases, from which these deploying personnel and equipment would originate, need an equivalent WMOG capacity to sustain the same rate of deployment. In this analysis, we assume that those bases' existing aerial port operations could suffice, or other resources from the en route system could be diverted to support this deployment.

[46] CR forces most definitely have other functions aside from merely supporting WMOG, but one of the CR's strengths is the ability to quickly stand up or expand capability and capacity at an airfield with no other U.S. presence, something that could be necessary in the operating environments we contemplate.

[47] *Parking MOG* is the maximum number of aircraft that can stay for longer periods (e.g., remain overnight). Orletsky, Brown, et al., 2023, discusses the types of MOG.

[48] The model is described in Orletsky, Brown, et al., 2023, Appendix E.

at a given base to simultaneously service aircraft varies by aircraft type. In this document, we report results for C-17s only for the WMOG demand and WMOG capacity in terms of widebody aircraft. In the technical appendixes, we include demand calculations for all aircraft types covered in this analysis.[49]

Figure 5.1 shows the total of the WMOGs required by airlifters at the forward (i.e., receiving) bases only, in the Pacific vignette. The WMOG demand is for C-17 aircraft; the Contingency Response Group capacity is for widebody aircraft. This assessment assumes that CR forces would support forward bases and some other USAF aerial port units could support the main operating base's WMOG needs (generic aerial port units are plentiful relative to total Contingency Response Group capacity).

As in the airlift analysis, we provide results for two extreme cases: one in which USAF must provide organic support for fully austere locations and 100 percent of the footprint must be airlifted from outside the theater and one in which the host nation can provide a significant amount of base support services. For each AB concept, we show the WMOGs required for deployment and employment phases. The number of bases to be supported is given next to each AB concept on the horizontal axis. The maximum WMOG demand is 14 for the cases analyzed.

Using data provided by AMC headquarters, we estimate the *authorized* WMOG capacity of AMC and PACAF's CR to be 27 widebody aircraft.[50] Our analysis of USAF manpower and personnel data suggest that CR units are, force-wide, manned at about 88 percent of authorizations on average (current as of 2019), bringing the total capacity down to about 23.[51] The true capacity of CR units is the *available* forces, which could be even lower than assigned forces. Thus, current CR forces, if fully marshaled, could support the *forward* WMOG required to rapidly deploy a single wing of F-35s in the most stressing of our AB cases (i.e., "Shell 6" in Figure 5.1).

---

[49] This is described in Orletsky, Brown, et al., 2023, Appendix F.

[50] These data were provided by AMC/A3MM on August 1, 2019, via email.

[51] This is based on 2019 manpower and personnel data obtained by RAND.

**Figure 5.1. Base WMOG Required Versus CR Capability**

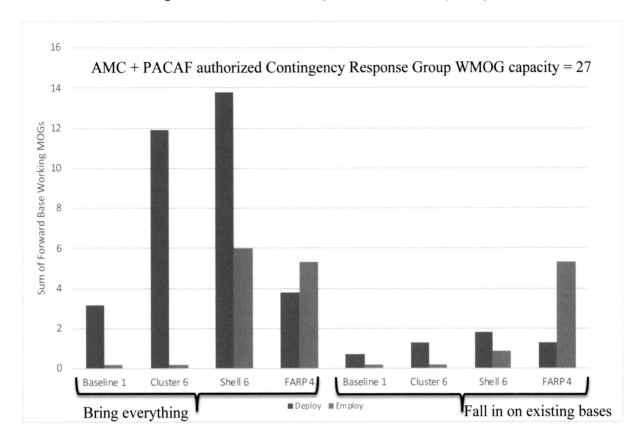

In reality, it is unlikely that USAF would have to provide entirely organic support to fully resourced demands at completely austere bases using standard airlift offload times (especially in such a high-threat environment). Figure 5.1 shows just how much alternative sources of supply (i.e., host-nation support, contract support, and prepositioning) can reduce the WMOG demand due to reduced footprint and airlift demand. Likewise, as our technical work shows, expedited offload techniques can also reduce the WMOG demand by a factor of 50–75 percent.[52] That would also make it tractable for the estimated current CR force capacity to support both forward and rear WMOG demands for one wing employing AB concepts in this vignette.

We can see from this limited discussion that the supply and demand for CR forces depends on many variables and assumptions, many outside AMC's control. AMC should engage to the maximum extent possible with PACAF (and other component major commands), USAF

---

[52] Orletsky, Brown, et al., 2023, uses data on available forces to calculate a more realistic capacity number and also shows numerous variants of the WMOG demand, as it is also sensitive to assumptions about expedited offload times, which can significantly reduce WMOG demands.

headquarters, and other stakeholders to understand the still-nascent demand signals from AB and similar concepts.[53]

## BOS

BOS includes such functional capabilities as civil engineering, security, communications, and medical support, and it supports forward operating locations for AB and any beddown. Although AMC provides BOS forces to forward deployments, it does not own the preponderance of forces: Other organizations, including USAF Logistics, Engineering and Force Protection, Air Force Installation and Mission Support Center (AFIMSC), and PACAF, have significant authority and responsibility for key decisions, including war reserve materiel investment and force packaging and presentation.[54] We present this analysis of BOS demands in AB environments to equip AMC leadership to enter broader discussions about how to support AB.

Past RAND research assessed the total force capacity of the agile combat support forces to support expeditionary operations. It found that the wartime capacity of the entire force is well above demands in the cases analyzed,[55] suggesting that around 25–30 squadron-sized forward bases could be supported by the current total force.[56] The AB concepts in this analysis contemplate only up to six fighter locations, far below the threshold of the previous analysis. As shown in Figure 3.2 as many as 15 tankers operating close in (depending on MDS) could be required to support fighters at close-in bases. Dividing those along the lines of six to eight tankers per base (about half of the traditional lines of 12–16 PAA per base) would require two or three tanker bases forward. Operating in three- or four-ship tanker deployments could require as many as six bases. The sum of fighter and tanker bases in the worst case would thus be 15. The current USAF-wide BOS personnel capacity would be sufficient to support one or two wings of fighters plus tanker support, with fairly demanding AB cases,[57] but there would be little capacity to support the remaining bases for the campaign. This finding assumes that USAF must provide complete organic support to austere bases. There are many ways USAF can offset the demand for BOS, as we explore later in this chapter.

---

[53] This assessment depends on our assumptions about the total time allotted to deployment; more time would result in a lower WMOG requirement. See Appendixes E and I (Orletsky, Brown, et al., 2023) for more detail regarding analysis of WMOG in this scenario.

[54] The first two of these has significant policy and other authorities, and PACAF has significant BOS forces relevant to AB and authority over its own prepositioned equipment stocks.

[55] Patrick Mills, John G. Drew, John A. Ausink, Daniel M. Romano, and Rachel Costello, *Balancing Agile Combat Support Manpower to Better Meet the Future Security Environment*, Santa Monica, Calif.: RAND Corporation, RR-337-AF, 2014.

[56] Mills et al., 2014. The limiting factors were found to be explosive ordnance disposal; chemical, biological, radiological, and nuclear; and firefighting.

[57] As described by Mills et al., 2014, with the assumptions used therein.

An additional challenge for BOS is that AB concepts often call for nontraditional force packaging to support deployment of very small size, short duration, or both. USAF has a de facto force packaging and equipping strategy that is designed around very different operating conditions from those of AB and related concepts.[58] The strategy assumes that presence will be robust and sustained; equipment sets need to be durable, so they can last for long-term deployments in punishing environments (e.g., deserts in the Middle East); and time and lift to deploy are fairly plentiful. The result is individual pieces of equipment, equipment sets, and entire force packages that are robust (i.e., providing significant capability and capacity for sustained durations) and positioned in a few consolidated locations. Although this arrangement makes maintenance and oversight efficient, it does not foster responsiveness and agility.

## Potential Enhancements

This section considers approaches to increase the capacity of, or reduce demand for, enablers and otherwise adapt the force to be more suitable to AB. Because of AMC's limited role in BOS, our BOS-related enhancements should be taken as pointing to promising directions, but there remains uncertainty about how far PACAF or USAF will move toward them.

### Altering MAF Force Packages to Better Accommodate AB Demands

To improve MAF support to AB, force packages could be (re)designed to better accommodate the demands of more dispersed or decoupled operations. This could better balance the tension between degrading performance of forward units and that of home-station units. Doing so would help planners proactively plan for and present forces for AB-type operations. Several factors could be varied to add granularity to force packages:

- **Duration:** Staffing and supplies for traditional combat aircraft maintenance UTCs are designed for 30 days of operations, but some AB concepts could require UTCs to operate for a much shorter duration (<24 hours), conducting only flightline sortie generation, akin to a FARP or drop-in location.
- **Package size:** Traditional UTC packages are typically designed and sized to perform a mix of maintenance actions (e.g., aircraft mission generation, on-aircraft repair, and off-aircraft repair) and to deploy in traditional lead-follow packages. To better support AB, units might be resourced to support smaller independent (i.e., lead) packages.

---

[58] See Patrick Mills, James A. Leftwich, Kristin Van Abel, and Jason Mastbaum, *Estimating Air Force Deployment Requirements for Lean Force Packages: A Methodology and Decision Support Tool Prototype*, Santa Monica, Calif.: RAND Corporation, RR-1855-AF, 2017; and Patrick Mills, James A. Leftwich, John G. Drew, Daniel P. Felten, Josh Girardini, John P. Godges, Michael J. Lostumbo, Anu Narayanan, Kristin Van Abel, Jonathan W. Welburn, and Anna Jean Wirth, *Building Agile Combat Support Competencies to Enable Evolving Adaptive Basing Concepts*, Santa Monica, Calif.: RAND Corporation, RR-4200-AF, 2020.

- **Multiple MDSs:** Maintenance personnel are generally certified on the weapon system owned by their current unit. To support AB operations, maintainers might need to be concurrently qualified and certified to work on different MDSs.

Whereas the internal structure of today's maintenance UTCs (including deployment echelons) incorporate some modularity appropriate for AB concepts (e.g., the en route support team and advanced echelon teams), AB-driven force packages would likely be built on combinations of the above factors, giving planners more options to tailor packages to various AB integrated basing structures.

*Expanding and Restructuring CR Capability and Capacity*

As discussed above, current CR forces, if fully marshaled, could support the *forward* WMOG required to rapidly deploy a single wing of F-35s in the most stressing of our AB cases (Figure 5.1), although there might not be sufficient CR capacity to support rapid deployment of more-demanding cases, including simultaneous support of both forward bases and main operating bases in our analytic cases. Many factors contribute to the WMOG demand, and the status of some of those factors is still quite unresolved. It is therefore difficult to state definitively how much AB the CR force could support. That said, increasing and expanding CR capability and capacity could help to support larger operations using AB.

CR units in USAF are already in the process of making or experimenting with two changes that would make them more suitable to the AB environment. The first is to change their structure to enable them to support more and smaller locations simultaneously. Recently, CR units have focused more on opening and establishing small numbers of large bases that require significant investment of time and manpower to prepare them for operations. The current direction USAF is taking is that each Contingency Response Group would have a nested structure of CR elements and CR teams, such that they could sustainably split up into smaller and smaller forces and provide support to more locations simultaneously, albeit at lower levels of capacity at each location. This would allow them more flexibility and ability to cover an expansive network of bases.

Another change some CR units are experimenting with is training and exercising with CAF maintenance and munitions maintenance personnel to enable CR units to base with CAF operations. CR units traditionally support only MAF operations, but given the current planning environment, there is an appetite to expand that. These capabilities might not ultimately be absorbed into CR units from an organize, train, and equip perspective, but there are a number of ways, institutionally, for those CAF capabilities to train and exercise and then deploy with traditional CR forces that are workable.

At the same time, CR forces are manned at about 88 percent of current authorizations, and their actual "available" capacity could be even lower. Fully manning these units is more a matter of personnel management (and institutional incentives) than additional funding, since the authorizations already exist. This would go some distance to increasing global capacity.

## Using Technology to Facilitate Airlift Offload and Reduce Time on Ground

In Chapter 4 we described how expedited offload techniques and new technologies can reduce the time airlifters spend on the ground, exposed to a threat. Some of the same enhancements, such as wheeled pallets and roll-off trucks/trailers, can also reduce the demand for specialized material handling equipment or operators—and thus the overall WMOG demand. By reducing traditional WMOG demand, such technologies or investments would enable airlift cargo offload to occur more rapidly, at more locations, in potentially more-austere environments. Exactly how much faster or more broadly this could be scaled and deployed is uncertain. Although the technologies described in Chapter 4 have already been fielded in one form or another (but not in USAF), more testing and experimentation would be necessary to establish how they would be incorporated into real-world units and operations to see what contributions they could make. AMC's involvement and investment would be required to further develop and field those capabilities.

## Cross-Training Personnel to Relieve Shortfalls and Improve Mobility

Cross-training is another idea being pursued in many corners of the USAF to attempt to better support AB. Sometimes cross-training is proposed to reduce the total footprint of a deployment, thereby increasing speed and responsiveness. Another benefit is to increase the capacity of the force by making certain skills more widely available. There are many possibilities, but potentially serious downsides and trade-offs that come with adding training and skills to airmen. Mills and coauthors enumerated some of these possibilities in the context of AB, but we focus on a few here.[59]

To address the potential shortfall in WMOG capacity (i.e., providing enough aerial port and material handling capacity), cross-training could add material handling and other mobility-related skills to personnel other than aerial porters. This could increase the WMOG capacity across the force. In some cases, flight engineers or loadmasters are trained to operate forklifts or other material handling equipment. It is possible for other agile combat support personnel to attain some of these skills, including transportation skills, load planning, joint inspection, and forklift operation. CR units already perform cross-training on these skills for most of their personnel, and their training regimens could serve as a template. USAF has been and continues to scrutinize the potential costs and benefits of cross-training (also called *multiskilling*). The analysis to date has not yet provided definitive estimates of which skills could be trained more broadly, nor at what cost, making it difficult to estimate how much of which demands could be relieved.

---

[59] Mills et al., 2020.

## Reshaping BOS Force Packaging and Force Presentation to Better Support AB

There is already movement across USAF to rethink and redesign force packages (and force presentation concepts) to better suit AB operations. This includes PACAF's agile combat employment concept, with tailored base packages; AFIMSC's Installation and Mission Support Weapons and Tactics (I-WEPTAC) working groups and combat support wing concept,[60] individual major commands' and flying wings' experiments and exercises,[61] and past RAND analysis.[62] Likewise, CR and special operations forces already have some more-tailored unit and equipment designs that may serve as templates.[63] These efforts to reimagine deployment force packages are already moving toward better support to AB and may have a mitigating influence on overall footprint and mobility. This finding applies to both maintenance and BOS. These efforts are still too early to quantify exactly what impacts they might have on AB demands for BOS.

## Relying on Nonorganic Sources of BOS Capability and Capacity

The above analysis of BOS requirements shows a worst-case scenario, in which the full complement of resources is required at most bases and USAF organic forces must provide and transport those resources. In reality, few expeditionary bases that USAF supports require that full complement to be provided organically by USAF. Many expeditionary locations have preexisting facilities that provide some or all of a given function, and host-nation militaries and joint forces also often provide equipment or personnel to partially offset USAF needs. Lynch and coauthors reviewed a number of base deployments from Joint Task Force–Noble Anvil in Kosovo, Operation Enduring Freedom in Afghanistan, and Operation Iraqi Freedom, describing some of the capabilities already at expeditionary locations, additional capabilities required, and processes and timelines to do so.[64] There are bases that require the full treatment (e.g., Bagram Air Base, Afghanistan, which was essentially built from scratch into a fully operational major location), but most bases required something less than that.

Although USAF often relies on host-nation support for certain functions, only certain base functions would be suitable for "outsourcing," and each has unique strengths, weaknesses, costs, and risks. For example, the United States regularly operates from mature partner-nation airfields

---

[60] Brian Bruckbauer, Steve Thomas, and Josh Hager, "Combat Support Wing," white paper, San Antonio, Tex.: Air Force Installation and Mission Support Center, Joint Base San Antonio, September 2017.

[61] Examples are PACAF's Arctic Agile Combat Employment exercise, USAFE's RAPID-X concept, and Global Strike Command's Bomber Task Force concept.

[62] See Mills, Leftwich, et al., 2017; Mills et al., 2020.

[63] For example, Air Force Special Operations Command has a bare base package called Air Rapid Response Kit that provides capabilities similar to Basic Expeditionary Airfield Resources (BEAR) but requiring a fraction of the lift.

[64] Kristin F. Lynch, John G. Drew, Robert S. Tripp, and Charles Robert Roll, Jr., *Supporting Air and Space Expeditionary Forces: Lessons from Operation Iraqi Freedom*, Santa Monica, Calif.: RAND Corporation, MG-193-AF, 2005.

that already have robust airfield operations, fuel support, or perimeter security. But some tasks would be too sensitive for non-U.S. military personnel to perform. At the same time, there is a question as to whether these alternative sources would be able to provide the capacity needed in the time required. Whether in a limited AB case or a broader campaign, joint, host-nation, or contract support could offset some of the deployment and thus airlift demand. Initiative for these decisions lies with PACAF and USAF.

Recognizing the importance of host-nation cooperation, China is working to use its soft, sharp, and hard power to convince and coerce America's regional allies to deny it military access and refuse cooperation. Given China's important trade relations with these states, Beijing has ample leverage with which to do so. USAF planners may need to work with other government agencies and local partners to determine what levels of support will be available in which contingencies and whether there is anything planners can do to encourage greater cooperation with local partners.

### *Expanding Prepositioned Equipment Stocks*

Recently, PACAF has developed a more or less standalone equipment prepositioning concept and posture strategies called Regional Base Cluster Package kits. USAF could also invest in additional theater equipment stocks to expand deployment capacity. Recent analysis suggests that USAF *already* faces shortfalls in its global inventory, let alone for expanding that inventory for any new, large-scale operating locations.[65] War reserve materiel has been chronically underfunded against previously validated requirements, whereas some AB concepts would call for multiplying the number of new locations and thus the total requirements. PACAF and USAFE have both been proposing large-scale expansions of their war reserve materiel equipment stocks, which suggests that they perceive even greater needs beyond their current requirements.[66] Even with force package redesign and relying on other sources of supply, purchasing and prepositioning additional equipment stocks could mitigate airlift demand.

---

[65] War reserve materiel inventory data from the 635th Supply Chain Operations Wing show that globally the "fill rate" of war reserve materiel (on-hand divided by authorized) is about 50–70 percent, depending on the command, with the average being about 62 percent by dollar value (data provided on February 16, 2016). The authorized amounts, dating from early 2016, are presumably based on legacy requirements—i.e., not accounting for AB or other similar concepts.

[66] USAFE–Air Forces Africa and PACAF headquarters are advocating to buy billions of dollars in new war reserve materiel, each under theater-unique concepts. USAFE's sets are referred to as the *deployable air base system* (DABS), and PACAF's are Regional Base Cluster Package kits. These massive purchases alone suggest that the component commanders discern significant shortfalls in their current war reserve materiel inventories to meet their wartime responsibilities.

## Conclusions

AB concepts challenge many of the assumptions that have long guided force packaging and equipping strategies, requiring the rapid establishment of small bases in dispersed and potentially austere locations for potentially short periods of activity. Although the scale of demand is difficult to predict, it is likely that existing maintenance packages, CR forces, and BOS capabilities would need to be expanded or restructured to provide the necessary flexibility and capacity. Some efforts are already under way: AMC should continue to pursue these initiatives; explore further promising enhancements to force packaging, training, and technologies; and work with USAF's Logistics, Engineering and Force Protection, AFIMSC, PACAF, and others to ensure that BOS resources are prepared to support AB operations.

# 6. Additional Issues Affecting the Mobility Air Forces

This chapter briefly identifies additional issues, outside the analytic scope of this project, that USAF should consider as it prepares mobility forces to support AB concepts in contested environments.

## C2 with Degraded or Unreliable Communications

Although not a major focus of this work, C2 is an important consideration in AB operations, for both the CAF and the MAF. As previously mentioned, the existing global airlift C2 system is already accustomed to making on-the-fly changes regarding airlift taskings reacting to dynamic changes in mission or user needs and mission diverts or changes for many reasons, such as weather, maintenance, or airfield issues. So-called in-system select is an existing method by which mobility C2 agencies redirect a mission in progress to satisfy a new, more urgent requirement.[67] This system depends on having reliable communications with ground-support agencies and crews, both on the ground and in the air, but is not currently well coordinated with CAF units. Effective AB will require dynamic, real-time coordination with CAF forces. One could imagine a "just-in-time" delivery mode, in which fighters and required support equipment could be redirected during an operation in response to an attack or other circumstance. Current operations and C2 structures are not in place for this level of real-time, dynamic interoperability.

As envisioned by PACAF and others, AB concepts will execute in a dynamic environment, where fighter crews may take off without knowing where they will land, instead having multiple options depending on the tactical situation. This could be a difficult C2 environment, depending on how the MAF goes about satisfying the requirement. One idea might be to routinely resupply an array of small bases to keep on-hand stock of fuel, ammunition, parts, and supplies at predetermined levels. In such a case, the MAF would not need to react as quickly to the day-to-day CAF operations. Such a system would be compatible with existing MAF C2 systems (assuming reliable communications). However, some AB concepts under consideration envision MAF C-17 or C-130 aircraft being lashed up with, for example, a two- or four-ship of F-35s, arriving at a FARP just in time to refuel and re-arm the fighters and then depart. This type of employment would require very close coordination between the MAF and CAF crews involved and would likely need to operate with a degree of independence from the 618th Air Operations Center (AOC) or theater Air Mobility Division.

---

[67] *In-system select* is a term used by the Tanker Airlift Control Center and aircrews when selecting an aircraft or sortie that is already on a mission or in the global air mobility "system" to do a higher-priority mission.

The above employment concept would require dependable communications between and among the MAF and the CAF. In a conflict with a near peer, it seems likely that both long- and potentially short-range communications could be degraded, compromised, or denied. Most MAF C2 systems run on unclassified networks that could be vulnerable to disruption or manipulation in a contested environment. In its extreme, C2 may need to take place using "old school" physical methods, such as hand-delivered mission-type paper orders. Decision authority in such a situation would likely need to be localized at the unit or even aircraft level. The local mobility commander would need to be in close proximity to their CAF counterpart. At present, MAF C2 nodes and crews do not routinely practice using alternate communication systems to transmit orders or plan missions. The pace of operations in such an environment, compounded with the flexibilities inherent in the AB concept, will likely require greater adaptability and tighter coordination between CAF and MAF C2 than exists today.

## Navigation

It is likely that traditional GPS and radio navigation beacons will be jammed, degraded, or even denied in a conflict with a near peer. During World War II, scores of U.S. military aircraft in the Pacific campaign went missing because they literally got lost over the ocean and crashed into the sea. Although today's aircraft are typically equipped with inertial navigation systems (INSs), aircrew and aircraft navigation systems are highly reliant on GPS for navigation, timing, and terrain avoidance. At present, C-17 and C-130J aircrew are not allowed (by policy) to airdrop without an accurate navigation solution. Recognizing this, several MAF units are now training their crews to operate without GPS. However, these techniques require crews to make reference to surface features by radar or visually and to input corrections into the aircraft navigation system. Progress notwithstanding, these techniques are ill suited to oceanic navigation. Further, it is possible that GPS guidance could be spoofed in ways not readily apparent to a nontrained aircrew. In such a case, the enemy could bias onboard navigation systems to fool aircrews into flying to places or in directions advantageous to itself. As a result, navigation difficulties in a contested environment may constrain, limit, and impede MAF warfighting operations. Training of crews to be suspicious of navigation drift and constantly comparing navigation solutions—not just the Kalman-filtered solution, which is often heavily weighted by GPS—may be required to better enable operations in a degraded environment.

## Real-Time Threat Warning

By and large, MAF aircraft are not equipped with the same real-time data links that CAF aircraft have. This presents two issues. First, mobility aircrew are at a severe threat-warning disadvantage, making operations in a contested environment more dangerous. Second, tight tactical coordination between the MAF and the CAF is more difficult and not nearly as efficient and effective as may be required to support some or many AB tactical employment concepts.

Real-time threat warning could have significant operational benefits, especially if coupled with CONOPs, such as engine running offloads at ramps near the end of a runway to allow mobility aircraft to flush on warning and be airborne in a few minutes.

## Culture

As a whole, the MAF has long been optimized for efficient operations in a permissive to low-threat environment. MAF procedures, policies, and even tactics are designed around centralized decisionmaking. Aircrew and ground crew are expected to operate "by the book" and to seek guidance or waivers when presented with unusual problems. Aircrew do not plan their own missions: That function is performed by flight managers located in the 618th AOC. Yet the types of conflict that AB is designed to handle will likely demand decentralized decisionmaking and self-initiated dynamic planning, all while operating in the kind of contested environment the MAF has not operated in before. Changing the culture to accommodate these needs may be the greatest adaptation required by the MAF.

## Local Access Politics

With the exception of the standoff concept, all of the basing concepts considered in this report require the use of local airfields and other facilities. Even a campaign waged from standoff bases could require access to other nations' airspace. Many of the options we have discussed to reduce the burden these basing arrangements place on the MAF, such as the use of ground transportation or prepositioned stocks, would require even greater host-nation engagement. In the past, even staunch American allies have sometimes denied USAF forces the use of their airspace or territory for particular missions, often because they feared economic or military retaliation.[68] Beijing has already begun using economic carrots and sticks to change the behavior of states in the region toward the United States and is likely to continue to do so in the future.[69]

## Conclusion

In addition to addressing the force structure and resourcing issues discussed throughout this report, USAF should further explore the C2, navigation, threat-warning, and culture issues that could complicate effective MAF support to AB operations in contested environments. Assuming

---

[68] Stacie L. Pettyjohn and Jennifer Kavanagh, *Access Granted: Political Challenges to the U.S. Overseas Military Presence, 1945–2014*, Santa Monica, Calif.: RAND Corporation, RR-1339-AF, 2016, pp. 23–24, 76–77, 108–109; Amy Austin Holmes, *Social Unrest and American Military Bases in Turkey and Germany Since 1945*, New York: Cambridge University Press, 2014, pp. 191–192.

[69] David Josef Volodzko, "China Wins Its War Against South Korea's U.S. THAAD Missile Shield—Without Firing a Shot," *South China Morning Post*, November 18, 2019. See Appendix B (Orletsky, Brackup, et al., 2023) for a more in-depth discussion of the political limits to basing access to implement the main operating base, cluster, shell game, and FARP/drop-in concepts.

that AB is the future of USAF operations, these factors need to be addressed and improved on if AB is to prove feasible. Many of these solutions could be addressed through enhanced training and experimentation. AMC should consider the required modifications to training to address these potential shortfalls.

# 7. Conclusions and Recommendations

AB is a complex solution to a complex problem. It will require new and more-flexible ways of supporting and employing combat power against more-capable adversaries than the United States has faced in recent years. As stakeholders throughout the USAF and joint communities consider the shape that AB could take and its implications for CAF force structure and concepts of operation, it is important to also consider the impact on critical supporting forces and specifically the MAF.

This report examined the potential impact of several plausible AB concepts on MAF force structure and resources. Below, we summarize our major conclusions and recommend next steps for the MAF as it prepares to meet the emerging challenges of AB.

## Conclusions

The NDS Summary highlighted important new strategic and operational challenges for the nation and called on the U.S. Department of Defense to innovate in response to those challenges. AB concepts are a central thrust of joint force innovation, and, given the uncertainty of the emerging operational environment, an adaptive MAF will be essential to the viability of joint AB. An adaptive MAF will therefore create significant national strategic advantage for the United States.

### *Sufficiency of Current MAF Capabilities*

Comparison of current capabilities with potential demands for a variety of AB concepts in a Pacific vignette suggests that MAF forces, as currently configured and resourced, would likely have difficulty supporting adaptive CAF operations in a contested environment. Major conclusions are as follows:

- Under most circumstances, base enablers (e.g., contingency response forces and base operation support) could support the AB cases analyzed, but an entire theater campaign would stress resources.
- Different AB concepts have different implications for the MAF. AB concepts that call for tankers to support CAF forces from standoff would greatly multiply the demand for tankers. Concepts that require fighters to move dynamically among different bases (e.g., shell game and FARP/drop-in) would be especially demanding for airlift during the employment phase. If bases must be set up without host-nation support or prepositioning of resources, the airlift need during the deployment phase would be greatly increased. Host-nation support and prepositioning resources would be critical to conducing these operations, given the current level of airlift capacity.

- Under most circumstances, the MAF can support small elements of CAF fighters (about ten two-ship CAPs total) using AB concepts with tanker standoff operations, assuming that about half of the total MAF fleet is devoted to this operation.
- MAF units are not sized or structured to support AB and related concepts: The USAF force packaging and equipping strategy is not designed to deploy in small packages at large scale.
- USAF-wide BOS personnel capacity can support the number of bases for the AB cases we analyzed, but prior research has found that supporting an entire theater campaign would stress some low-density agile combat support functional areas.[70]
- Basing access is inherently political and uncertain, making lean and inherently mobile operations desirable.
- Additional issues, outside the analytic scope of this report, could complicate MAF support to AB concepts. These include the need for closer and more-flexible C2 coordination between the CAF and the MAF, reliance on communications and navigation systems that could be vulnerable in contested environment, absence of real-time threat warning for MAF aircraft, and a MAF culture that is designed around centralized decisionmaking.

### *Potential Enhancements to Better Support AB Concepts*

Several enhancements could potentially reduce the above shortfalls to varying degrees. The following enhancements are worth further consideration, experimentation, and cost-effectiveness analysis:

- Tankers will likely need to operate closer to the fight to meet large demands.
- Minimizing forward ground times and operating from multiple forward bases could enhance tanker survivability. Reducing the time tankers spend on the ground (through high UTE rates and other techniques) would reduce threat exposure, allow tankers to operate from closer in, and thereby greatly lower fleetwide demand to support AB operations. The tankers would then return to standoff bases as required for major maintenance.
- Tanker force extension (i.e., "buddy tanking") could modestly reduce the overall number of tankers required (up to about 25 percent) to support CAF operations from standoff.
- A hypothetical "super tanker" with much larger capacity than existing or planned tankers could reduce the demand for tankers operating from standoff.
- When possible, ground transportation could reduce the intratheater airlift requirement.
- New systems (advanced technology) and CONOPs could shorten aircraft ground times, enhance logistical operations, and cut the deployed footprint.
- Cross-training personnel offers significant potential to reduce deployed footprint, relieve shortfalls, and improve deployment and employment timelines.
- Institutionalizing structural changes to CR units that enable them to support numerous small locations would then enable them to better support dispersed and fluid AB operations.

---

[70] Mills et al., 2014.

- Increasing and expanding CR capability and capacity would enable these forces to support more than just one large operation using AB.
- Use of external fuel tanks and higher maximum weight allowance could increase C-130J-30 capability and thereby reduce airlift demand, depending on the operating distances.
- Joint, host-nation, and contract support and prepositioning are required to offset some of the large airlift demand.
- Seeking agreements in advance with potential partners, such as the predesignated bases in the Philippines' Enhanced Defense Cooperation Agreement, is highly desirable.

## Recommendations

The above conclusions indicate that AB concepts being considered across USAF could have significant impact on the MAF. We offer the following recommendations, cognizant of the fact that USAF and joint communities are still considering the precise shape that AB could take and how it could be implemented. The recommendations are presented in a logical order of implementation, starting with the need to integrate MAF considerations into AB discussions taking place today. Once this is under way, AMC can begin to experiment with different approaches to best support the AB concepts being developed. On the basis of its findings, AMC would then undertake cost-effectiveness analyses and eventual procurement of new capabilities.

**1. AMC should enhance integration with USAF and joint organizations to ensure that the air mobility perspective is included in discussions of potential AB concepts.** In USAF, this would mean better coordination with such organizations as USAF's Air Force Warfighting Integration Center, PACAF, USAFE, and U.S. Air Forces Central Command. Coordination should extend to joint organizations looking at the larger concepts of forward force maneuver and posture resilience (of which AB is a part) to ensure that these concepts are feasible from a mobility perspective. This should include working with U.S. Transportation Command, the U.S. Army, and the U.S. Navy to identify how transportation assets could best be used under different circumstances to support AB. It should also extend to Army headquarters, U.S. Army Pacific, and other Army components to consider positioning (including afloat) Army truck company equipment sets in potential operating areas. These discussions should consider other services providing assets that could self-redeploy or increase total equipment numbers to reduce the air mobility burden on *base moves*. Examples include air defense, security personnel, and heavy equipment (e.g., air base repair). Training and full integration with these other organizations could also be required. Further, more integration is likely required in the C2 constructs, not only between the MAF and the CAF but with other services to operate dynamically under wartime conditions. This includes coordination with U.S. and allied governments to enhance the potential for desirable U.S. basing and to better understand the impact on operations of certain basing locations being restricted or unavailable due to Chinese use of hard, soft, or sharp power.

**2. USAF should undertake experiments and exercises to develop new CONOPs that allow the MAF to more effectively support AB operations.** Throughout this analysis we have seen that changes to current tactics, techniques, and procedures can increase the ability of the MAF to support larger CAF forces that are using AB. In many cases, our analysis showed a significant operational benefit of certain changes (e.g., reducing ground time, reducing support footprint, operating tankers forward), but many potential issues and pitfalls may lie in the implementation. AMC should conduct experiments and exercises to identify and understand how best to implement good ideas to enhance operations while taking prudent risks. These could involve AMC alone or could take place in the context of Red Flag or other USAF exercises. These could include an actual drop-in/FARP exercise with the CAF or a tabletop exercise to flesh out C2 constructs different from the highly centralized control of the 618th AOC or the Air Mobility Division.[71]

**3. AMC should completely review rules to determine what new regulations are needed for AB operations in contested environments.** Many of the enhancements discussed in this report will likely require changes in Air Force instructions and other rules that may limit effectiveness in the types of conflict envisioned here. Although waivers can (and are) granted to accomplish missions, a new way of operating could be required to effectively conduct wide-scale operations against a near-peer competitor. A real-time, commander-by-commander waiver process would be impractical and undesirable in a fast-paced, high-threat conflict. We suggest that the evaluation include Air Force instructions, maintenance procedures, base operations procedures, and safety regulations to identify where prudent risk can be taken to increase the effectiveness of MAF operations in this context. Required procedures (e.g., maintenance and fuel simultaneously), maintenance items (e.g., mission critical versus defer), and base procedures (e.g., cross-training of personnel, reliance on host-nation support) should be reviewed to develop an AMC AB warfighting CONOP that is trained and implemented, if required, to maximize the MAF's capability to support AB concepts. This CONOP must be flexible enough to account for geopolitical factors and adversary soft-power actions that could make basing posture uncertain.

**4. USAF should consider how different equipment and technologies, coupled with new CONOPs, could better enable the MAF to support AB operations.** Enhanced technology and improved equipment suited to this potential fight is a critical part of the solution. Base enablers designed to speed ground operations while reducing deployed footprint (e.g., autopallets) show considerable promise and should be considered and evaluated. Further, communications and navigation equipment designed to operate in a degraded environment, coupled with better integration with the MAF and joint or combined entities, would better enable flexible, dynamic, and more-efficient forward operations. Some CONOPs would be enabled by advanced technology and should be explored. For example, a reliable missile warning system, coupled with ground operations near the end of a runway, could permit MAF aircraft flushing on warning of an impending attack.

---

[71] We thank our RAND colleague Anthony Rosello for these specific ideas.

**5. USAF should conduct a cost-effectiveness analysis to identify the best approaches to implementing the new CONOPs.** Our final recommendation builds on the above. Some level of technology acquisition will be needed to enable the CONOPs identified through experiments and exercises. In some cases, the costs will be relatively small, given the improvement in the MAF's ability to support AB concepts. These cases should be highlighted and considered for immediate implementation. In other cases, USAF should work with labs and other organizations to determine which technologies should be pursued, given the estimated costs and expected payoffs. This analysis should provide a road map of research, development, and acquisition to most cost-effectively develop the needed AB capability.

Meeting the challenges of near-peer adversaries requires flexibility and innovation from all parts of USAF. AB has the potential to make combat forces more survivable and effective in the most-challenging threat environments that USAF has had to face in decades. But combat power will only ever be as effective as the enabling capabilities that keep it fueled, supplied, maintained, and operational. Mobility must be part of any discussion of future basing concepts, and the MAF itself must be prepared to adapt and evolve so it can continue to provide effective support to combat forces.

# Abbreviations

| | |
|---|---|
| AB | adaptive basing |
| AFIMSC | Air Force Installation and Mission Support Center |
| AMC | Air Mobility Command |
| AOC | Air Operations Center |
| BOS | base operating support |
| C2 | command and control |
| CAF | combat air forces |
| CAP | combat air patrol |
| CONOP | concept of operations |
| CR | contingency response |
| DCA | defensive counterair |
| FARP | forward area refueling point |
| ISA | International Standard Atmosphere |
| MAF | Mobility Air Forces |
| MDS | mission design series |
| MOG | maximum on ground |
| MTV | medium tactical vehicle |
| NDS | National Defense Strategy |
| PAA | primary aircraft authorized |
| PACAF | Pacific Air Forces |
| PLS | Palletized Load System |
| USAF | U.S. Air Force |
| USAFE | U.S. Air Forces in Europe |
| UTC | unit type code |
| UTE | utilization |
| WMOG | working maximum on ground |

# Bibliography

"72% of Okinawa Voters Oppose Work off Henoko for U.S. Base," *Asahi Shimbun*, February 25, 2019. As of March 18, 2022:
https://www.asahi.com/ajw/articles/13054550

Aero Specialties Ground Support Equipment, "2183 Caster Deck Pallet Trailer," webpage, undated. As of September 26, 2019:
https://www.aerospecialties.com/aviation-ground-support-equipment-gse-products/aviation-baggage-cargo-service-equipment/2183-caster-deck-pallet-trailer

Aglionby, John, "African Union Accuses China of Hacking Headquarters," *Financial Times*, January 29, 2019.

Air Force Instruction 25-101, *Logistics Staff: Air Force War Reserve Materiel (WRM) Policies and Guidance*, Washington, D.C.: U.S. Department of the Air Force, January 14, 2015.

Air Force Manual 11-2C-130J, *Flying Operations C-130J Operations Procedures*, Vol. 3, Washington, D.C.: U.S. Department of the Air Force, July 17, 2019.

Air Force Pamphlet 10-1403, *Air Mobility Planning Factors*, Washington, D.C.: U.S. Department of the Air Force, October 24, 2018.

Air Mobility Command, "Halverson Loader," fact sheet, June 1 2016a. As of September 26, 2019:
https://www.amc.af.mil/About-Us/Fact-Sheets/Display/Article/144024/halvorsen-loader

———, "Tunner 60K Loader," fact sheet, June 1, 2016b. As of September 26, 2019:
https://www.amc.af.mil/About-Us/Fact-Sheets/Display/Article/144023/tunner-60k-loader/

Air Mobility Command Instruction 10-202, *Mission Management and Reliability Reporting System (MMRRS)*, Vol. 6, Washington, D.C.: U.S. Air Force, March 15, 2011.

Anderson, Charles R., "Guadalcanal," brochure, U.S. Army Center for Military History, October 2003.

Armstrong, Peter F. C., "The Battle of Guadalcanal: A 50-Year Retrospective," *Marine Corps Gazette*, Vol. 76, No. 8, August 1992.

Baldwin, David A., *Power and International Relations: A Conceptual Approach*, Princeton, N.J.: Princeton University Press, 2016.

Bever, Lindsey, "U.S. Marine Convicted of Killing Transgender Filipina," *Washington Post*, December 1, 2015.

Bolger, Daniel P., "Scenes from an Unfinished War: Low-Intensity Conflict in Korea, 1966–1969," Leavenworth Papers, U.S. Army Command and General Staff College, No. 19, July 1991. As of February 21, 2019:
https://www.armyupress.army.mil/Portals/7/combat-studies-institute/csi-books/Scenes-Froman-Unfinished-War.pdf

Bolinger, James, "Japan Stalled in Hunt to Replace Iwo Jima as Site for U.S. Carrier-Landing Practice," *Stars and Stripes*, May 24, 2019. As of March 18, 2022:
https://www.stripes.com/theaters/asia_pacific/japan-stalled-in-hunt-to-replace-iwo-jima-as-site-for-us-carrier-landing-practice-1.582709

Borlaza, Gregario C., Michael Cullinane, Carolina G. Hernandez, and the editors of Encyclopedia Britannica, "Philippines," *Encyclopedia Britannica*, June 28, 2019. As of July 9, 2019:
https://www.britannica.com/place/Philippines

Bowe, Alexander, *China's Overseas United Front Work: Background and Implications for the United States*, Washington, D.C.: U.S.-China Economic and Security Review Commission, August 24, 2018. As of August 14, 2019:
https://www.uscc.gov/sites/default/files/Research/China%27s%20Overseas%20United%20Front%20Work%20-%20Background%20and%20Implications%20for%20US_final_0.pdf

Brown, Charles Q., Jr., Bradley D. Spacy, and Charles G. Glover III, "Untethered Operations: Rapid Mobility and Forward Basing Are Keys to Airpower's Success in the Antiaccess/Area-Denial Environment," *Air and Space Power Journal*, May–June 2015.

Brown, Erin, "Burlington City Council Votes to Oppose 'Nuclear-Capable Aircraft' in Burlington," WCAX 3, August 13, 2009. As of August 14, 2019:
https://www.wcax.com/content/news/Burlington-City-Council-votes-to-formally-denounce-presence-of-F35-jets-538710571.html

Bruckbauer, Brian, Steve Thomas, and Josh Hager, "Combat Support Wing," white paper, San Antonio, Tex.: Air Force Installation and Mission Support Center, Joint Base San Antonio, September 2017.

Bu Aeri, <추미애 평화협정 체결해도 주한미군 주둔해야> ["Chu Mi-ae, 'Even If a Treaty Is Signed, U.S. Forces Must Remain in Korea'"], *Asian Economy*, May 2, 2018.

Byers, Adrian Rainier, *Air Supply Operations in the China-Burma-India Theater Between 1942 and 1945*, thesis, Fort Leavenworth, Kan.: U.S. Army Command and General Staff College, 2010.

Calder, Kent E., *Embattled Garrisons: Comparative Base Politics and American Globalism*, Princeton, N.J.: Princeton University Press, 2007.

Camp, Richard, "The Cactus Air Force's Humble Home," *Naval History*, Vol. 31, No. 4, August 2017a.

———, "Flying in the Eye of the Guadalcanal Storm," *Naval History*, Vol. 31, No. 4, August 2017b.

Choi He-suk, "Moon Accuses Gwangju Uprising Deniers of Undermining Foundations of Korea," *Korea Herald*, February 18, 2019. As of July 15, 2019: http://www.koreaherald.com/view.php?ud=20190218000645

Cliff, Roger, Mark Burles, Michael S. Chase, Derek Eaton, and Kevin L. Pollpeter, *Entering the Dragon's Lair: Chinese Antiaccess Strategies and Their Implications for the United States*, Santa Monica, Calif.: RAND Corporation, MG-524-AF, 2007. As of August 12, 2019: https://www.rand.org/pubs/monographs/MG524.html

Cooley, Alexander, *Base Politics: Democratic Change and the U.S. Military Overseas*, Ithaca, N.Y.: Cornell University Press, 2008.

Cooley, Alexander, and Jonathan Hopkin, "Base Closings: The Rise and Decline of the U.S. Military Basses Issue in Spain, 1975–2005," *International Political Science Review*, Vol. 34, No. 4, September 2010, pp. 494–513.

Cooley, Alexander, and Daniel H. Nexon, "The Empire Will Compensate You': The Structural Dynamics of the U.S. Overseas Basing Network," *Perspectives on Politics*, Vol. 11, No. 4, December 2013, pp. 1034–1050.

Corr, Anders, "China's Threat of War Against Philippines Is Baseless Scare Tactic," *Forbes*, May 20, 2017. As of July 9, 2019: https://www.forbes.com/sites/anderscorr/2017/05/20/chinas-threat-of-war-against-philippines-is-baseless-scare-tactic/#6f45d54a39f9

Correll, John T., "The Matterhorn Missions," *Air Force Magazine*, March 2009.

Craven, Wesley Frank, and James Lea Cate, eds., *The Army Air Forces in World War II*: Vol. IV, *The Pacific, Guadalcanal to Saipan*, Chicago: University of Chicago Press, 1950.

———, *The Army Air Forces in World War II*: Vol. V, *The Pacific: Matterhorn to Nagasaki, June 1944 to August 1995*, Washington, D.C.: Office of Air Force History, 1983.

DeBlois, Bradley, Thomas Light, Daniel M. Romano, Michael Boito, John G. Drew, Paul Emslie, Michael Kennedy, Kathryn O'Connor, and Jonathan William Welburn, *Options for Enhancing the Effectiveness of Maintenance Force Structure: Examining the Decline in KC-135 Availability*, Santa Monica, Calif.: RAND Corporation, 2020, Not available to the general public.

Envall, H. D. P., "Underplaying the 'Okinawa Card': How Japan Negotiates Its Alliance with the United States," *Australian Journal of International Affairs*, Vol. 67, No. 4, July 2013, pp. 383–402.

Feis, Herbert, *China Tangle: The American Effort in China from Pearl Harbor to the Marshall Mission*, Princeton, N.J.: Princeton University Press, 1953.

Field Manual 4-02.10, *Theater Hospitalization*, Washington, D.C.: U.S. Department of the Army, January 2005.

Field Manual 4-20.116/Technical Order 13C7-1-13, *Airdrop of Supplies and Equipment: Reference Data for Airdrop Platform Loads*, Washington, D.C.: U.S. Department of the Army and U.S. Department of the Air Force, May 2006.

Field Manual 55-15, *Transportation Reference Data*, Washington, D.C.: U.S. Department of the Army, 1997.

Flight Manual Technical Order 1C-130(C)J-1-1, *Performance Data USAF Series C-130J (Long) Aircraft*, Washington, D.C.: U.S. Department of the Air Force, change 2, July 1, 2011.

Fox, William J., "Building the Guadalcanal Airbase," *Marine Corps Gazette*, March 1944.

Frank, Richard, *Guadalcanal: The Definitive Account of the Landmark Battle*, New York: Penguin Books, 1990.

Gamel, Kim, "New Commander Takes Charge at Army's New Home on Korean Peninsula," *Stars and Stripes*, June 27, 2019. As of July 16, 2019: https://www.stripes.com/news/pacific/new-commander-takes-charge-at-army-s-new-home-on-korean-peninsula-1.587805

Glosserman, Brad, and Scott A. Snyder, *The Japan-South Korea Identity Clash: East Asian Security and the United States*, New York: Columbia University Press, 2015.

Goldsmith, Benjamin E., and Yusaku Horiuchi, "In Search of Soft Power: Does Foreign Public Opinion Matter for U.S. Foreign Policy?" *World Politics*, Vol. 64, No. 3, July 2012, pp. 555–585.

Gorman, G. Scott, *Endgame in the Pacific: Complexity, Strategy, and the B-29*, Maxwell, Ala.: Air University Press, 2000.

Green, Alex E. S., Deborah S. Green, and Richard L. Francis, "OR Forum—a Glimpse at an Operation Analyst's World War II: 'Report on the Combat Performance of the Remote Control Turrets of B-29 Aircraft,'" *Operations Research*, Vol. 63, No. 2, March–April 2015, pp. 262–268.

Gutierrez, Jason, "Philippine Official, Fearing War with China, Seeks Review of U.S. Treaty," *New York Times*, March 5, 2019.

Hamilton-Hart, Natasha, *Hard Interests, Soft Illusions: Southeast Asia and American Power*, Ithaca, N.Y.: Cornell University Press, 2012.

Harper, Jon, "U.S. Air Force Preparing for 'High Volume' Operations in Europe," *National Defense Magazine*, April 5, 2016.

Harris, Harry B., Jr., "Logistics Officers Association Symposium," speech delivered at the U.S. Pacific Command of the Logistic Officer Association Symposium, National Harbor, Md., October 13, 2016. As of September 29, 2017:
www.pacom.mil/Media/Speeches-Testimony/Article/974913/logistics-officer-association-symposium/

"Has Duterte's China Pivot Backfired?" *Asia Times*, April 17, 2019. As of July 9, 2019:
https://www.asiatimes.com/2019/04/opinion/has-dutertes-china-pivot-backfired

Haulman, Daniel L., *The U.S. Army Air Forces in World War II: Hitting Home; The Air Offensive Against Japan*, Washington, D.C.: Air Force History and Museums Program, 1999.

Hess, Gary R., "With Friends Like These: Waging War and Seeking 'More Flags,'" in David L. Anderson and John Ernst, eds., *The War That Never Ends: New Perspectives on the Vietnam War*, Lexington: University Press of Kentucky, 2007.

Heydarian, Richard, "Duterte Heads to Beijing on Tide of Philippine Dissent over 'Meek and Humble' South China Sea Policy," *South China Morning Post*, August 18, 2019. As of August 20, 2019:
https://www.scmp.com/news/china/diplomacy/article/3023078/duterte-heads-beijing-tide-philippine-dissent-over-meek-and

Hillestad, R. J., *Dyna-METRIC: Dynamic Multi-Echelon Technique for Recoverable Item Control*, Santa Monica, Calif.: RAND Corporation, R-2785-AF, 1982. As of May 25, 2021:
https://www.rand.org/pubs/reports/R2785.html

Holmes, Amy Austin, *Social Unrest and American Military Bases in Turkey and Germany Since 1945*, New York: Cambridge University Press, 2014.

Holyk, Gregory G., "Paper Tiger? Chinese Soft Power in East Asia," *Political Science Quarterly*, Vol. 126, No. 2, Summer 2011, pp. 223–254.

Hook, Glenn D., "Intersecting Risks and Governing Okinawa: American Bases and the Unfinished War," *Japan Forum*, Vol. 22, Nos. 1–2, 2010, pp. 195–217.

Hook, Glenn D., and Key-yong Son, "A Tale of Two 'Alliances': Internal Threats and Networked Civil Society in Japan-U.S. and South Korea-U.S. Base Politics," *Pacific Focus*, Vol. 28, No. 1, April 2013, pp. 17–42.

Hornfischer, James D., *Neptune's Inferno: The U.S. Navy at Guadalcanal*, New York: Bantam Books, 2011.

Hsiao, Russell, "A Preliminary Survey of CCP Influence Operations in Singapore," *China Brief*, Vol. 19, No. 13, 2019.

Jaeger, Sheila Miyoshi, *Brothers at War*, New York: W. W. Norton and Company, 2013.

Jeong Seok-Hwan, <한국등, 美에 송개서한 'PVID원칙 견지해달라'> ["Liberty Korea Party Sends an Open Letter to the U.S. Requesting They Persevere with PVID"], *Economics Daily*, May 17, 2018.

Johnson, E. R., "Operation Matterhorn," *Aviation History*, July 2003.

Johnson, Keith, "Why Are Japan and South Korea at Each Other's Throats?" *Foreign Policy*, July 15, 2019. As of July 17, 2019:
https://foreignpolicy.com/2019/07/15/why-are-japan-and-south-korea-in-a-trade-fight-moon-abe-chips-wwii/

Joint Publication 3-0, *Joint Operations*, incorporating change 1, Washington, D.C.: Joint Chiefs of Staff, October 22, 2018.

Joint Publication 3-17, *Air Mobility Operations*, Washington, D.C.: Joint Chiefs of Staff, February 5, 2019.

Kagotani, Koji, and Yuki Yanai, "External Threats, U.S. Bases, and Prudent Voters in Okinawa," *International Relations of the Asia-Pacific*, Vol. 14, No. 1, January 2014, pp. 91–115.

Katigbak, Jose, "US, Philippines Agree on 5 Base Locations Under EDCA," *Philippine Star*, March 19, 2016. As of July 9, 2019:
https://www.philstar.com/headlines/2016/03/19/1564662/us-philippines-agree-5-base-locations-under-edca

Kawato, Yuko, *Protests Against U.S. Military Base Policy in Asia: Persuasion and Its Limits*, Stanford, Calif.: Stanford University Press, 2015.

Keaney, Thomas, and Eliot Cohen, *Gulf War Air Power Survey*: Vol. V, *A Statistical Compendium and Chronology*, Washington, D.C.: U.S. Department of the Air Force, 1993.

Killingsworth, Paul, Lionel A. Galway, Eiichi Kamiya, Brian Nichiporuk, Robert S. Tripp, and James C. Wendt, *Flexbasing: Achieving Global Presence for Expeditionary Aerospace Forces*, Santa Monica, Calif.: RAND Corporation, MR-1113-AF, 2000. As of May 20, 2021:
https://www.rand.org/pubs/monograph_reports/MR1113.html

Kim, Claudia J., "War Over Framing: Base Politics in South Korea," *Pacific Review*, Vol. 30, No. 3, 2017, pp. 309–327.

Koji Kagotani and Yuki Yanai, "External Threats, U.S. Bases, and Prudent Voters in Okinawa," *International Relations of the Asia-Pacific*, Vol. 14, No. 1, January 2014, pp. 91–115.

Kornylak Corporation, "40K Loader/Unloader Specialty Vehicles for Air Cargo Handling Systems," webpage, undated. As of September 26, 2019:
http://kornylak.com/vehicles/40k-loader.html

Kusumoto, Hana, "Air Force Will Pay Japanese City $7 Million over Noise Complaints," *War Is Boring*, June 10, 2019. As of July 30, 2019:
https://warisboring.com/air-force-will-pay-japanese-city-7-million-over-noise-complaints/

Kyodo News, "Okinawa Files Another Lawsuit over U.S. Base Landfill Work," *Japan Times*, July 17, 2019. As of July 30, 2019:
https://www.japantimes.co.jp/news/2019/07/17/national/crime-legal/okinawa-files-another-lawsuit-u-s-base-landfill-work/#.XUDdGjp7kit

Lane, Greg, "Operation Watchtower: Soldiers Were Key in World War II's First U.S. Offensive," *Army Magazine*, May 2017.

Lankford, Mark, "The Case for Micro-Basing Logistics for the AirSea Battle," Maxwell Air Force Base, Ala.: Air University, March 2011.

Lee-Brago, Pia, "U.S. to Remain Philippines' Only Military Ally," *Philippine Star*, April 8, 2019. As of July 9, 2019:
https://www.philstar.com/headlines/2019/04/08/1908199/us-remain-philippines-only-military-ally

Lema, Karen, and Martin Petty, "Two Years After Philippines' Pivot, Duterte Still Waiting on China Dividend," Reuters, November 18, 2018. As of August 21, 2019:
https://www.reuters.com/article/us-philippines-china-analysis/two-years-after-philippines-pivot-duterte-still-waiting-on-china-dividend-idUSKCN1NN0UO

LeMay, Curtis, and Bill Yenne, *Superfortress: The Boeing B-29 and American Airpower in World War II*, Yardley, Pa.: Westholme Publishing, 1988.

Loewenthal, Robyn, "Seabee Days: The 50th Anniversary of the Group Will Be Celebrated in Festivities June 4–6 at the Port Hueneme Base," *Los Angeles Times*, May 28, 1992.

Lostumbo, Michael J., Michael J. McNerney, Eric Peltz, Derek Eaton, David R. Frelinger, Victoria A. Greenfield, John Halliday, Patrick Mills, Bruce R. Nardulli, Stacie L. Pettyjohn, Jerry M. Sollinger, and Stephen M. Worman, *Overseas Basing of U.S. Military Forces: An Assessment of Relative Costs and Strategic Benefits*, Santa Monica, Calif.: RAND Corporation, RR-201-OSD, 2013. As of May 20, 2021:
https://www.rand.org/pubs/research_reports/RR201.html

Lynch, Kristin F., John G. Drew, Robert S. Tripp, and Charles Robert Roll, Jr., *Supporting Air and Space Expeditionary Forces: Lessons from Operation Iraqi Freedom*, Santa Monica, Calif.: RAND Corporation, MG-193-AF, 2005. As of August 2, 2020:
https://www.rand.org/pubs/monographs/MG193.html

Marine Corps Warfighting Publication 3-21.2, *Aviation Logistics*, Washington, D.C.: U.S. Marine Corps, October 21, 2002.

Marsh, Carol, "A History of the Navy Civil Engineer Corps, 1867–2007," Historian's Office, Navy Facilities Engineering Command, April 2007.

McLaughlin, Timothy, "A U.S. Ally Is Turning to China to 'Build, Build, Build,'" *The Atlantic*, May 8, 2019. As of July 9, 2019:
https://www.theatlantic.com/international/archive/2019/05/philippines-us-ally-china-investment/588829/

Mersky, Peter B., *Time of the Aces: Marine Pilots in the Solomons*, Washington, D.C.: Marine Corps Historical Center, 1993.

Miller, John, Jr., "Crisis on Guadalcanal," *Military Affairs*, Vol. 11, No. 4, 1947.

———, *Guadalcanal: The First Offensive*, Washington, D.C.: Center of Military History, U.S. Army, 1995.

Mills, Patrick, John G. Drew, John A. Ausink, Daniel M. Romano, and Rachel Costello, *Balancing Agile Combat Support Manpower to Better Meet the Future Security Environment*, Santa Monica, Calif.: RAND Corporation, RR-337-AF, 2014. As of May 20, 2021:
https://www.rand.org/pubs/research_reports/RR337.html

Mills, Patrick, James A. Leftwich, John G. Drew, Daniel P. Felten, Josh Girardini, John P. Godges, Michael J. Lostumbo, Anu Narayanan, Kristin Van Abel, Jonathan William Welburn, and Anna Jean Wirth, *Building Agile Combat Support Competencies to Enable Evolving Adaptive Basing Concepts*, Santa Monica, Calif.: RAND Corporation, RR-4200-AF, 2020. As of May 20, 2021:
https://www.rand.org/pubs/research_reports/RR4200.html

Mills, Patrick, James A. Leftwich, Kristin Van Abel, and Jason Mastbaum, *Estimating Air Force Deployment Requirements for Lean Force Packages: A Methodology and Decision Support Tool Prototype*, Santa Monica, Calif.: RAND Corporation, RR-1855-AF, 2017. As of May 21, 2021:
https://www.rand.org/pubs/research_reports/RR1855.html

Mills, Patrick, Caolionn O'Connell, Kristin F. Lynch, John G. Drew, Louis W. Miller, Kristin Van Abel, Peter Buryk, Carter C. Price, and Paul Emslie, *Analysis of U.S. Air Force Surge Capacity for Aircraft Availability, Costs, Challenges, and Opportunities*, Santa Monica, Calif.: RAND Corporation, 2017, Not available to the general public.

Morrison, Charles E., and Daniel Chinen, *Millennial+ Voices in Okinawa: An Inquiry into the Attitudes of Young Adults Toward the Presence of U.S. Bases*, Honolulu: East-West Center, April 2019. As of July 31, 2019:
https://www.eastwestcenter.org/publications/millennial-voices-in-okinawa-inquiry-the-attitudes-young-adults-toward-the-presence-us

Moseley, T. Michael, *Operation Iraqi Freedom—by the Numbers*, Shaw Air Force Base, S.C.: U.S. Central Command Air Forces, April 30, 2003.

Mourdoukoutas, Panos, "Malaysia Is Standing Up to China," *Forbes*, July 19, 2019. As of August 13, 2019:
https://www.forbes.com/sites/panosmourdoukoutas/2019/07/19/malaysia-is-standing-up-to-china/#758baa8573c3

Mulcahy, Paul, webpage for U.S. trailers, *Paul Mulcahy's Pages*, undated. As of September 26, 2019:
https://www.pmulcahy.com/trailers/us_trailers.htm

Nye, Joseph S., Jr., *Soft Power*, New York: Public Affairs, 2004.

———, "Get Smart: Combining Hard and Soft Power," *Foreign Affairs*, Vol. 88, No. 4, July–August 2009, pp. 160–163.

———, "How Sharp Power Threatens Soft Power: The Right and Wrong Ways to Respond to Authoritarian Influence," *Foreign Affairs*, January 24, 2018. As of August 14, 2019:
https://www.foreignaffairs.com/articles/china/2018-01-24/how-sharp-power-threatens-soft-power

O'Brien, Cyril J., "The Coastwatchers," *Leatherneck*, November 1992.

O'Connell, John F., "What Might Have Been—XX Bomber Command's B-29 Offensive Against Japanese Oil Supplies in the Netherlands East Indies and Borneo," *Air Power History*, Vol. 64, No. 1, Spring 2017, pp. 41–46.

Office of the Secretary of Defense, *Annual Report to Congress: Military and Security Developments Involving the People's Republic of China 2019*, Washington, D.C.: U.S. Department of Defense, May 2, 2019.

O'Neal, Michael, *Expeditionary Air Forces' Roots in the Past: Cactus Air Force*, Maxwell, Ala.: Air University, 1999.

Onishi, Norimitsu, "Okinawans Protest Japan's Plan to Revise Bitter Chapter of World War II," *New York Times*, October 7, 2007.

Orletsky, David T., Julia Brackup, Christian Curriden, Adam R. Grissom, Patrick Mills, and Robert A. Guffey, *How Can the Mobility Air Forces Better Support Adaptive Basing? Appendixes A–C, Supporting Analyses of Adaptive Basing, Soft Power, and Historical Case Studies*, Santa Monica, Calif.: RAND Corporation, RR-A1125-2, 2023. As of January 17, 2023:
www.rand.org/pubs/research_reports/RRA1125-2.html

Orletsky, David T., Jeffrey S. Brown, Bradley DeBlois, Patrick Mills, Daniel M. Norton, and Robert A. Guffey, *How Can the Mobility Air Forces Better Support Adaptive Basing? Appendixes D–I, Supporting Analyses of Tankers, Airlift, and Base Enablers*, Santa Monica, Calif.: RAND Corporation, 2023, Not available to the general public.

Orletsky, David T., Michael Kennedy, Bradley DeBlois, Daniel M. Norton, Richard Mason, Dahlia Anne Goldfeld, Andrew Karode, Jeff Hagen, James S. Chow, James Williams, Alexander C. Hou, and Michael J. Lostumbo, *Options to Enhance Air Mobility in Anti-Access/Area Denial Environments*, Santa Monica, Calif.: RAND Corporation, 2022, Not available to the general public.

OshKosh Defense Contractor, homepage, undated. As of May 20, 2021:
https://oshkoshdefense.com

Pettyjohn, Stacie L., and Jennifer Kavanagh, *Access Granted: Political Challenges to the U.S. Overseas Military Presence, 1945–2014*, Santa Monica, Calif.: RAND Corporation, RR-1339-AF, 2016. As of June 27, 2019:
https://www.rand.org/pubs/research_reports/RR1339.html

Pew Research Center, Global Indicators Database, undated. As of August 13, 2019:
https://www.pewresearch.org/global/database

Philippart, Jeff D., *The Expeditionary Airfield as a Center of Gravity: Henderson Field during the Guadalcanal Campaign (August 1942–February 1943)*, Maxwell Air Force Base, Ala.: Air University Press, 2004.

Postrado, Leonard, "EDCA Prevails," *Manila Bulletin*, January 13, 2016. As of July 9, 2019:
https://web.archive.org/web/20160305211340/http:/www.mb.com.ph/edca-prevails

Poushter, Jacob, and Caldwell Bishop, "People in the Philippines Still Favor U.S. over China, but Gap Is Narrowing," Pew Research Center, September 21, 2017. As of July 9, 2019:
https://www.pewresearch.org/global/2017/09/21/people-in-the-philippines-still-favor-u-s-over-china-but-gap-is-narrowing

Priebe, Miranda, Alan J. Vick, Jacob L. Heim, and Meagan L. Smith, *Distributed Operations in a Contested Environment: Implications for USAF Force Presentation*, Santa Monica, Calif.: RAND Corporation, RR-2959-AF, 2019. As of July 12, 2021:
https://www.rand.org/pubs/research_reports/RR2959.html

Reif, Kingston, "Moon Reverses THAAD Decision," Arms Control Association, September 2017. As of July 17, 2019:
https://www.armscontrol.org/act/2017-09/news/moon-reverses-thaad-decision

Rein, Chris, "Guadalcanal: A Case Study for Multi-Domain Battle," *Military Review*, May–June 2018.

Rempfer, Kyle, "U.S., Filipino, and Aussie Forces Conduct Premier Military Exercise, but Don't Mention China," *Military Times*, April 11, 2019. As of July 9, 2019:
https://www.militarytimes.com/news/your-military/2019/04/11/us-filipino-and-aussie-forces-conduct-premier-military-exercise-but-dont-mention-china

Ridler, Keith, "Air Force Disputes Lawsuit to Stop Urban Training in Idaho," *Air Force Times*, June 8, 2019. As of August 14, 2019:
https://www.airforcetimes.com/news/your-air-force/2019/06/08/air-force-disputes-lawsuit-to-stop-urban-training-in-idaho

Robles, Raissa, "When Xi Meets Duterte: Is the China-Philippines Honeymoon Over?" *South China Morning Post*, August 13, 2019. As of August 20, 2019:
https://www.scmp.com/news/asia/diplomacy/article/3022429/when-xi-meets-duterte-china-philippines-honeymoon-over

Sanftleben, Kurt A., *The Unofficial Joint Medical Officers' Handbook*, 2nd ed., Bethesda, Md.: Uniformed Services University of the Health Sciences, 1997.

Schanz, Marc V., "Rapid Raptor Package," *Air Force Magazine*, September 27, 2013.

Shambaugh, David, "China's Soft-Power Push: The Search for Respect," *Foreign Affairs*, Vol. 94, No. 4, July–August 2015, pp. 99–107.

Sherrod, Robert, *History of the Marine Corps Aviation in WWII*, Washington, D.C.: Combat Forces Press, 1952.

Smith, Sheila A., *Shifting Terrain: The Domestic Politics of the U.S. Military Presence in Asia*, Honolulu: East-West Center, March 2006. As of July 9, 2019:
https://www.eastwestcenter.org/publications/shifting-terrain-domestic-politics-us-military-presence-asia

Snow, Shawn, "Philippine Commando Video Shows Marawi in Ruins After Liberation from ISIS," *Military Times*, December 4, 2017. As of July 9, 2019: https://www.militarytimes.com/flashpoints/2017/12/04/philippine-commando-video-shows-marawi-in-ruins-after-liberation-from-isis

Snyder, Glenn H., *Alliance Politics*, Ithaca, N.Y.: Cornell University Press, 1997.

Soft Power 30, homepage, undated. As of August 13, 2019: https://softpower30.com

Spinetta, Lawrence, "The Other Cactus Air Force," *Aviation History*, Vol. 25, No. 5, May 2015.

System Planning and Analysis, Inc., *Distributed Short Take-Off Vertical Landing (STOVL) Operations: An Initial Look at Concept Development and Feasibility Final Report*, Washington, D.C.: February 2014.

Technical Manual 4-48.03/Marine Corps Reference Publication 4-11.3C/Technical Order 13C7-1-11, *Airdrop of Supplies and Equipment: Rigging Containers*, Washington, D.C.: U.S. Department of the Army, U.S. Marine Corps, and U.S. Department of the Air Force, March 2016.

Technical Manual 4-48.15/Marine Corps Reference Publication 4-11.3A/Technical Order 13C7-1-171, *Airdrop of Supplies and Equipment: Rigging Ammunition Systems*, Washington, D.C.: U.S. Department of the Army, U.S. Marine Corps, and U.S. Department of the Air Force, March 2016.

Technical Manual 4-48.18/Technical Order 13C7-1-19, *Airdrop of Supplies and Equipment: Rigging Forward Area Refueling Equipment (FARE) and Advanced Aviation Forward Area Refueling Systems (AAFARS), Fuel Drums*, Washington, D.C.: U.S. Department of the Army and U.S. Department of the Air Force, March 15, 2016.

Tripp, Robert S., Alan J. Vick, Jacob L. Heim, and James A. Leftwich, *Increasing Air Base Resilience to Missile Attacks: Lessons Learned from RAND Analyses on Combat Operations in Denied Environments*, Santa Monica, Calif.: RAND Corporation, 2022, Not available to the general public.

Tsygankov, Andrei P., "If Not by Tanks Then by Banks? The Role of Soft Power in Putin's Foreign Policy," *Europe-Asia Studies*, Vol. 58, No. 7, pp. 1079–1099.

U.S. Air Force, "F-35A Lightning II," fact sheet, April 11, 2014. As of September 26, 2019: https://www.af.mil/About-Us/Fact-Sheets/Display/Article/478441/f-35a-lightning-ii-conventional-takeoff-and-landing-variant

U.S. Army, *Army 2023 Leader*, Washington, D.C., 2017.

U.S. Army Combined Arms Support Command, "Equipment Annex," in *Sustainment Force Structure Book*, Fort Lee, Va., 2018.

U.S. Department of Defense, *Summary of the 2018 National Defense Strategy of the United States of America, Sharpening the American Military's Competitive Edge*, Washington, D.C., 2018.

Vine, David, "No Bases? Assessing the Impact of Social Movements Challenging U.S. Foreign Military Bases," *Current Anthropology*, Vol. 60, Suppl. 19, February 2019.

Volodzko, David Josef, "China Wins Its War Against South Korea's U.S. THAAD Missile Shield—Without Firing a Shot," South China Morning Post, November 18, 2019. As of July 17, 2019:
https://www.scmp.com/week-asia/geopolitics/article/2120452/china-wins-its-war-against-south-koreas-us-thaad-missile

Walker, Christopher, "What Is 'Sharp Power'?" *Journal of Democracy*, Vol. 29, No. 3, July 2018, pp. 9–23.

Walker, Christopher, and Jessica Ludwig, "The Meaning of Sharp Power: How Authoritarian States Project Influence," *Foreign Affairs*, November 16, 2017. As of August 12, 2019:
https://www.foreignaffairs.com/articles/china/2017-11-16/meaning-sharp-power

Westcott, Ben, and Brad Lendon, "Duterte Threatens 'Suicide Mission' If Beijing Oversteps in South China Sea," CNN, April 5, 2019. As of July 9, 2019:
https://www.cnn.com/2019/04/05/asia/south-china-sea-duterte-beijing-intl/index.html

Wike, Richard, Bruce Stokes, Jacob Poushter, Laura Silver, Janell Fetterolf, and Kat Devlin, *Trump's International Ratings Remain Low, Especially Among Key Allies*, Washington, D.C.: Pew Research Center, October 1, 2018.

Willmott, H. P, "Guadalcanal: The Naval Campaign," *Joint Force Quarterly*, Autumn 1993, pp. 98–106.

Wilson, Ernest J., III, "Hard Power, Soft Power, Smart Power," *Annals of the American Academy of Political and Social Science*, Vol. 616, No. 1, March 2008, pp. 110–124.

Winnefeld, James A., and Dana J. Johnson, *Joint Air Operations: Pursuit of Unity in Command and Control, 1942–1991*, Annapolis, Md.: Naval Institute Press, 1993.

Working Group on Chinese Influence Activities in the United States, *Chinese Influence and American Interests*, Stanford, Calif.: Hoover Institution Press, 2018.

Yeo, Andrew, *Activists, Alliances, and Anti-U.S. Base Protests*, New York: Cambridge University Press, 2011.

Yoo, Hyon Joo, "The Korea-U.S. Alliance as a Source of Creeping Tension: A Korean Perspective," *Asian Perspective*, Vol. 36, No. 2, April–June 2012, pp. 331–351.